Only GOD
Can Give You
the POWER to Get
WEALTH
...That Will Last Forever!

To: Rhonda Fox

From: Odell Young Jr.

" God Bless "

Only GOD

Can Give You

the POWER to Get

WEALTH

...That Will Last Forever!

Odell Young, Jr.

Servante Publishers
Palmetto, Georgia

Only God Can Give You the Power to Get Wealth!
By Odell Young, Jr.

Edited by G. Lynne Alston-Leonard

Published by: Servante Publishers
513 Scott Circle
Palmetto, GA 30268

Scripture quotations, unless noted are from the New King James Version ©1982, by Thomas Nelson, Inc. Bibliographical References included.

How to Order:
Additional copies of this book can be purchased through Servante Publishers. Contact us for more information by:

Phone: (404) 319-0913
Fax: (770) 969-7711
Email: servantepublishers@earthlink.net

ISBN-10: 0-615-31158-X
ISBN-13: 978-0-615-31158-6

Cover design by Dana Taylor

Printed in the United States of America

DEDICATION

I asked God to allow His thoughts to inspire my thoughts to write the pages of this book. God answered my prayers. When the ideas began to flow, I could hardly write fast enough to capture every thought! I went into a speedwriting mode not to miss any thoughts that God was giving me.

I do not take any credit for the writing of this book, for I am only an instrument, and a tool for God to use however He desires, to fulfill His purpose and plan for my life. In this case, God needed to get these thoughts on paper for many believers to read and profit by. Therefore, in saying this, I give God the glory for He alone deserves the glory, the honor, the praise, and the thanks. Thank you Father! I performed the work by researching the Bible; as I was instructed by the Spirit to put what God gave me into this book form.

At this juncture, I would like to recognize my Savior and the royal titles He is known by. In Isaiah 9:6, it says, "He is the Son: His name is Wonderful! His name is Counselor! He is the Mighty God! He is the Everlasting Father! He is the Prince of Peace!"

I dedicate this book to the Great "I AM," Jesus Christ, My Savior and Lord.

> *"To Him who is able to keep us from falling and to present us before His Glorious presence without fault and with great joy — to the only God our Savior, be glory, majesty, power and authority, through Jesus Christ our Lord, before all ages, now and forevermore! Amen."*
> — JUDE 24 & 25(NIV)

Contents

Dedication   v

Acknowledgements   xi

Preface   xii

Introduction   xiv

CHAPTER 1: WEALTH IN YOUR LIFE   1
The "God kind" of wealth   2
Your desires for life   6
Possibilities for your life   11
Taking action for your life   12

CHAPTER 2: YOUR VISION FOR WEALTH   15
Always have an "I can" attitude   19
Programming your mind to win   22

CHAPTER 3: ACHIEVING EXCELLENCE FOR WEALTH   25
What God thinks of His children?   30
The right attitude for life   32
Why God created you in His image   34

CHAPTER 4: WEALTH AND LOVING OTHERS   37
Pride and humility   41
A "God" mindset   44

CHAPTER 5: POWER AND WEALTH   47
In Christ you can do great things   49
God has an assignment for you   51
Know what you want and you will get it   54

CHAPTER 6: WAITING ON GOD FOR WEALTH   57
Meditation   62
Problems are inevitable   63
Satan—the enemy of getting wealth God's way   65

CHAPTER 7:   COMMITMENT AND WEALTH   67
             Focusing your life   71
             How to stay happy and young forever   73
             Giving to the work of God   75

CHAPTER 8:   SETTING GOALS FOR WEALTH   79
             Imagination   83
             Let God direct your path and plans for life   84

CHAPTER 9:   PAYING THE PRICE FOR WEALTH   87
             Living with courage   90
             Developing good habits   94
             Procrastination in your life   95

CHAPTER 10: PREPARING FOR WEALTH   97
             The bible is a success manual   99
             You are a winner in Christ   101

CHAPTER 11: YOUR SELF-IMAGE AND WEALTH   103
             What do you think about you?   106
             To be born again   107
             God made you to last forever   109

CHAPTER 12: RIGHTEOUS THOUGHTS FOR WEALTH   111
             Facing life with confidence   116
             How to start each day   119
             Enthusiasm in your life   120

CHAPTER 13: WEALTH COMES WITH WISDOM   123
             God's plan for your life   125
             Your spiritual growth   126
             You are in the family of God   127

CHAPTER 14: BUILDING RELATIONSHIPS FOR WEALTH   129
             Enjoyment in your life   132
             The power of prayer in your life   135
             Everything begins with God   138

CHAPTER 15: DILIGENCE AND WEALTH   141
            God is committed to your success   144
            Persistence throughout your life   145
            Facing burnout   147

CHAPTER 16: WEALTH REQUIRES THINKING BIG   151
            Facing adversities in your life   155
            Facing your fears   158
            Consider the poor   160

CHAPTER 17: STRENGTH IN CHARACTER AND WEALTH   163
            Facing failure in your life   165
            Prosperity is your right   169
            The boldness in you   171

CHAPTER 18: WEALTH AND LEADERSHIP   173
            Trusting in God   177
            Your purpose in life   181
            Facing obstacles in life   183

CHAPTER 19: WEALTH AND GOD'S PROMISES TO YOU   185
            Facing hardships in your life   188
            Facing disappointments in life   190

CHAPTER 20: GOD'S COMMITMENT TO YOUR SUCCESS   191
            Self-control in your life   198
            Your faith walk in life   200
            What the bible says about money   203

CHAPTER 21: YOUR THOUGHTS AND IDEAS FOR WEALTH   207
            Discover who you are "In Christ"   209
            Never quit on your dreams   212
            You should have victory in everything   213

Conclusion   217

Bibliography   221

About the Author   223

ACKNOWLEDGEMENTS

I would like to recognize and say thank you to the following people who helped to make this book a reality.

To my lovely wife, Delores, who is my heart and joy sent by God. We both knew from the beginning that God assigned us to each other and blessed us to bring three beautiful children into this world.

Delores diligently reviewed and typed this manuscript. She always takes on any task and does it with excellence as though she is doing it for the Lord, for in fact, she truly is.

To my children, Angela, DeAnn, and Kevin, I love you with all my heart. Seeing how God has blessed my life to be their father, inspired me even more to write this book because it will be a success manual for them. I pray constantly for God to watch over them.

This is the legacy that Delores and I would like to leave for our children; that they would follow Jesus for He has been a beacon light to show us the way when the way was uncertain and sometimes scary.

To Michael Coley, a servant of God, sent to be my mentor in Christ Jesus. God brought us together via telephone while I was pursuing a business venture. God continues to reveal the secret things of His kingdom to Michael. I believe that Michael is a man after God's heart. Michael has dedicated his life to the assignment that God has given him. May God continue to bless him and his lovely wife Venetta and his precious daughter Shiloah. My family and I are truly blessed by God to have Michael in our lives.

To Creed Pannell, Jr., a brother in Christ, who is an exceptional man of faith and diligence. God himself brought us together to perform wonderful works for His glory.

PREFACE

The poet Kahlil Gibran wrote:

"Your children are not your children.
They are the sons and daughters of Life's longing for itself.
They come through you but not from you.
And though they are with you, yet they belong not to you.
You may give them your love but not your thoughts.
For they have their own thoughts.
You may house their bodies but not their souls,
For their souls dwell in the house of tomorrow,
which you cannot visit, not even in your dreams..." (Gibran 1923)

These words remind us that we are first and foremost, God's children. As I have continued to grow in my faith with God, I have come to realize that my relationship with God should not be any different than my earthly relationships—as grandson, son, and father.

As parents, we have rules and guidelines for our children to live by. Rules that are designed to help our children learn to govern themselves according to moral, ethical, and socially acceptable standards. If there were no rules, our children would not know their limitations as children, gain understanding of our expectations as parents, develop a sense of priorities, or begin to learn and establish limitations and standards for themselves. Without rules, they would never learn or experience the consequences of being disobedient.

If I told my son or daughter, at the age of ten years old, to come in the house before dark, it was for a good reason—to protect them and keep them from harm. If they decided not to do so, they would have disobeyed the house rule. Had I not told them when to come in, they would not have necessarily been in disobedience, because that rule was never established in the household.

If my children were to continue to disrespect the house rule, I would have no choice but to discipline them. They would need to be reminded of "who was in control and responsible for them" to emphasize the importance and seriousness of obeying the rules set forth by their parents. Their discipline would usually be associated with taking away a privilege they enjoyed, such as grounding them from playing outside with their friends for a week. While on punishment, my children would also not receive any additional rewards for positive or "good behavior" during that time period.

Why should you expect anything different as a child of God? If you are to receive any of the rewards that God has intended for each of us, you, too must come to understand that God, our Heavenly Father, treats all of us in a similar way. If you are obedient to God's Word, you will be richly rewarded with abundant wealth. If you are in a state of disobedience, you will not be rewarded with His many blessings until you change your habits and align your life according to His Word.

If you do not know His Word, however, you are still guilty of disobeying His Word because God's Word tells us to "study to show thyself approved." When you study God's Word, you gain understanding of the areas you are not obeying. You can, however, make the proper changes through prayer, humility, faith, forgiveness or whatever the need be to continue to receive God's blessings.

A WORD TO THE READER:

The messages throughout this book are designed to assist you, as a believer, to align your lifestyle with the Word of God so that you will be rewarded by your Heavenly Father for adherence and obedience to His Word—just as you reward your children for obedience and adherence to your word. There are requirements and conditions that must be met to receive wealth from God.

As you read this book, keep in mind that you must be a born again child of God, seeking to know him as your personal Savior. Throughout each chapter there are "Thoughts to meditate upon" that are intended to reinforce each chapter's main theme, and to help you prepare for the abundant life God has promised each of us.

Only God has the power to release wealth into your life when you operate on faith, and trust in God and his Holy Word. It is my prayer that you discover the knowledge needed to meet God's requirements for receiving His promises of wealth in your life.

Remember, just as you are a parent to your children, our Heavenly Father is the ultimate parent of each of us. Everything begins with God. He is your source, and your life. Honor Him with thanksgiving daily— as you would have your children honor and respect you. Just as it gives you joy to reward your children, know that it gives Him greater joy to reward you..

He lives in each of us.

INTRODUCTION

When God made the heavens and the earth, He also established laws that would govern man's destiny. These laws work for and against us depending on our frame of reference. These laws will always work, just as the consistency of the law of gravity.

One of God's established laws introduced to me years ago is the law of preparation. It is written:

"A man's gift makes room for him, and brings him before great men." (Proverbs 18:16) In laic terms, this could mean, "When the student is ready, the teacher will appear."

My venture into real estate began years ago when I read that seventy five percent of all millionaires made their first million dollars in some form of real estate investing. This planted the seed in my mind to pursue real estate as a way to build wealth.

I began to prepare myself by reading many books on real estate. This process continued for at least two years. By the time, I felt I had prepared enough to begin my venture into real estate; I did not have the money to make real estate investments. Instead, I decided to get involved in the renovation of single-family houses. I organized a crew of people who could handle any type of home renovation, and took responsibility for the marketing and sales of our services. I placed many flyers in various locations. About two weeks later, a person called me who wanted home repairs. I made an appointment to see this person and took an installer with me.

After we finished the repairs, the person pulled me aside and told me he had over $100,000 in savings at the bank. He went further to ask if I would be his partner in real estate. I agreed, with only a handshake. I was able to locate our first investment property for $14,000. We spent $28,000 for renovations, and later sold the property for $69,000. We were on our way to becoming two profitable investors. After the first investment, I discovered opportunities to profit at least $20,000 per property.

What was the law I found myself obeying? "When the student is ready, the teacher will appear." I had prepared myself by reading real estate books for months.

I did not know where the investment funds would come, but I knew that I had to prepare myself for this real estate venture. I left the rest of my vision to God. I believed He was the one who planted the seed for real estate in my thoughts over the years.

When you come to terms with the fact that God is the ultimate owner of the world and everything in it, you should seek God first, and seek a prosperous life second. Since God owns everything, He will decide whether you get wealth and keep it, or get wealth and do not keep it. There is a difference.

This book was written to share with you, a believer, how to get wealth God's way. When you get wealth God's way, two things are assured: God will give you wealth with no trouble attached, and He will give you wealth to keep indefinitely.

God simply wants you to trust Him, and seek to attain wealth the right way. As a believer, you must put God first in your life. There is no other way. Only God can give you the power to get wealth!

Let me also say this about "getting wealth." The book considers wealth from a biblical perspective. Wealth is not limited to currency. Wealth, in its entirety, represents all of God's blessings—food, water, health, sun, peace, love, happiness, joy, as well as financial success.

All wealth flows from Him. He is the ultimate provider of all gain. God has simply assigned each of us to be stewards of all His assets. Wealth will come to you once God's Word abides in you, and you abide in God. God will open Heaven's door to you as an obedient child, and give you the desires of your heart.

1

WEALTH IN YOUR LIFE

"I traverse the way of righteousness, in the midst of the paths of justice, that I may cause those who love Me to inherit wealth that I may fill their treasures."

—PROVERBS 8:20-21

Webster's Dictionary defines "wealth" as having a large amount of money, property, riches—a great abundance of anything. The Bible defines wealth as "the ability to experience and enjoy God's blessings." The child of God who knows God as Savior, has more wealth compared to a rich man that does not know God.

The accumulation of wealth is the most challenging, exciting undertaking there is. Focus your energy and discipline on making money. Everyone should want financial freedom. Regardless of how many books you have read on making money, there are more "money making ideas" in the Bible than in all the other books combined. And remember, you should never equate income with wealth. Income is what you make; wealth is what you own. Capitol is money used to make more money.

The "God kind" of wealth

I believe that God wants His children to be wealthy, not by the world's way, but by His way. The Bible speaks of wealth in the hands of believers as a blessing from God.

It is written:

"He who did not spare His own son, but delivered him up for us all, how shall He not with him also freely give us ALL things?"
— Romans 8:32

"I have come that they may have life, and that they may have it more abundantly."
— John 10:10

"A good man leaves an inheritance to his children's children, but the wealth of the sinner is stored up for the righteous."
— Proverbs 13:22

It is impossible for man to get wealth on his own without the help of God. It is God who must enable a person to acquire wealth.

"And you shall remember the Lord your God, for it is He who gives you power to get wealth that He may establish His covenant which He swore to your fathers, as it is this day."

— DEUTERONOMY 8:18

"...that I may cause those who love Me to inherit wealth, that I may fill their treasures."

— PROVERBS 8:21

"Praise the Lord, blessed is the man who fears the Lord, who delights greatly in His commands. His descendents will be mighty (successful) on earth. The generation of the upright will be blessed, wealth and riches will be in his home."

— PSALM 112:1-3

It is not good to have wealth or to pursue wealth without God in your life. God is the Source of ALL blessings. All wealth comes from God. We must use our possessions for God's purpose.

I believe that wealth gained without the "Blessing of God" is only temporary. There is a "story" that has circulated for years about many of this country's fortunate sons:

In 1923, six of the wealthiest men in the United States met at a hotel in Chicago. The combined wealth of these men was more than the funds in the entire United States Treasury. The six men were:

Charles M. Schwab—President of the largest steel company. He died penniless.

Richard Whitney—President of the N.Y. Stock Exchange.
Sentenced to prison for embezzlement. Released from prison,
only to be banned from dealing in securities industry.

Albert Bacon Fall—U.S. secretary of the interior under President Warren G. Harding. Sentenced to prison in 1929. Pardoned from prison after nine months. Died penniless several years later.

Jesse Livermore—Greatest bear on Wall Street. He committed suicide.

Ivan Kreuger—Head of World's Greatest Monopoly. He committed suicide.

Leon Fraser—President of a bank. He committed suicide.
(NA 2007)

While there are probably many lessons that can be learned from the actual recordings of the lives, gains, and losses of these men, one should certainly ask, "what place did God hold in the lives of these men?" It is my belief that monetary wealth and gain came before God, and their losses resulted because they did not get wealth God's way.

IT IS WRITTEN:

"For what profit is it to a man if he gains the whole
world and loses his own soul; or what will a man give in
exchange for his soul?
— MATTHEW 16:26

"For all can see that wise men die; the foolish and the
senseless alike perish and leave their wealth to others."
— PSALM 49:10(NIV)

God wants His children to have wealth and an abundant life. However, He does not want wealth to have us. Remember, it is God who gives us the power to get wealth (Deut. 8:18), but we must pursue wealth with a "God consciousness."

When God allows us to acquire wealth, we must use it to glorify Him.

IT IS WRITTEN:

"Wealth and riches will be in his house, and his righteousness endures forever."

—PSALM 112:3

God offers instructions to the rich.

IT IS WRITTEN:

"Command those who are rich in this present world not to be arrogant nor to put their hope in wealth, which is so uncertain, but to put their hope in God, who richly provides us with everything for our enjoyment. Command them to do good, to be rich in good deeds, and to be generous and willing to share. In this way they will lay up treasure for themselves as a firm foundation for the coming age, so that they may take hold of the life that is Truly Life."

—1 TIMOTHY 6:17-19(NIV)

THOUGHTS TO MEDITATE UPON
TO PREPARE FOR GOD'S ABUNDANT LIFE:

- You must know exactly what you want, this is your vision. Write it down.
- You must see yourself already in possession of your dream.
- Ask God for wisdom and His help.
- Set goals for the attainment.
- Take action.

Your desires for life

God will always keep His promise to the believer. You must remain obedient to Him. He will honor your request as long as your request is His will for you. You can always depend on God.

He wants us to depend on Him alone. God wants us, "His children" to have the best in everything. God delights in making us happy when we totally depend on Him.

IT IS WRITTEN:

"Delight yourself in the Lord, and He shall give you the desires of your heart."
—PSALM 37:4

All of God's children have desires. God has ALL POWER to give you your desires, but your desires must be good for you (and humanity) in God's view. Otherwise, He will not grant your request.

God knows what we desire even before we ask Him. He knows

what is best for us and He knows the plans He has for us. Some common desires among humankind are to be in good health, to acquire material things, to find the right mate, to own a business or find the right job, belong to the right church, to have good friends, attend the right school or college, and/or obtain financial stability.

Your desires, however, must fit into His purpose. As you grow in your relationship with God, you may often find that your desires may change over time.

For example, there are certain things I desired last year but have no desire for today. My biggest desire today is to please God and do His will. My desires today extend beyond the United States to other parts of the world. One of my desires is to support needy children in other countries.

Any burning desire, backed with faith can lift a person from any station in life to a place that can touch the lives of many people all over the world. It is God's desire for us to help feed the poor, spread the gospel, and help others no matter where they live.

This is God's business. When we take care of God's business FIRST, our business will be taken care of. This is the power of God.

It occurred to me, about one year ago, that God himself places desires in our hearts. You may think, at the time, that your desires belong to you. Actually, it may be a desire that God wants you to pursue—a desire He wants you to realize.

Remember, God has power to interject thoughts and desires into your mind. God made you, and He can control that which He made at any given time.

When you have a "God consciousness," you have God's power. At that point, you are in harmony with the Creator of this vast universe.

God said in His Word that He wants us to "imitate Him." What does it mean—"to imitate Him?"

In Genesis chapter one, God "SPOKE" to the universe and things happened! Can you speak to your situation and cause things to happen also? Yes! When you "SPEAK" God's Word over your circumstances, you give His Word voice. Therefore, you are imitating Him.

It is written:

"So Jesus said to them, because of your unbelief; for assuredly, I say to you, if you have faith as a mustard seed, you will say to this mountain, move from here to there, and it will move; and nothing will be impossible for you."
—MATTHEW 17:20

Remember, it takes no more effort to think big thoughts than to think little thoughts. We can serve more people by thinking big thoughts. God is a big thinker. We must become big thinkers also. Remember what God says in His Word.

It is written:

"Therefore I urge you, imitate Me."
— 1 CORINTHIANS 4:16

You can have anything in life you desire as long as it is within the will of God for your life and purpose. God himself places many of the desires that we have in our minds. We need God's help to make the desires a reality.

No one can live without God. He made us that way. We are creatures of the Creator. In Him we live.

It is written:

"For in Him we live and move and have our being."
—ACTS 17:28A(NIV)

We are the offspring of God, which means in many ways, we are just like God. We can do great things in this life with Him by our side, but apart from Him, we can do nothing.

Go for those things that are in your heart. Think big and achieve great things. God has put the power in you to do amazing things, so do not think small of yourself like many people do. You were created to do godly things and to affect the people around you in a big way.

Remember, little thoughts lead to little achievements and big thoughts lead to big achievements.

To do anything significant in life, you must first have desires. God could have placed these desires in your mind. You honor God when you act upon your desires. Allow God to get the glory by making your desires a reality.

A desire, when harnessed, is power. Failure to follow your desire, to do what you want to do most, paves the way to being just average.

Every human being on this earth has some form of desire. All of us dream of what we want to do. But only a few actually go after the desire that is in us. Most people will allow the desire to dissipate into thin air.

Amazingly, as we pursue our desire for God, He gives us our desires. When we put Him first—we put His desires before our own wants and needs. In doing so, we have honored Him with delight.

IT IS WRITTEN:

"Delight yourself also in the Lord, and He will give you the desires of your heart."

—PSALM 37:4

9

Pleasing God is not a chore, rather it becomes a joy done out of humility and thankfulness. Our desires change from satisfying ourselves to pleasing God. God desires to fill us with pleasure, joy, and happiness forever.

As we pursue God, He will fulfill the desires He has given us. God places desires in us, which many times, we think that these desires are strictly our own. Yet, as God meets our desires, our longing for Him continues to grow. Our desired goals remain the same, yet there are less of us and more of God.

IT IS WRITTEN:

"You will show me the path of life; in Your presence is fullness of joy! At your right hand are pleasures forever more."

—PSALM 16:11

THOUGHTS TO MEDITATE UPON
TO PREPARE FOR GOD'S ABUNDANT LIFE:

- Some thoughts are from God. He may have created some of your desires.
- You are able to speak your desires into existence because God said you could.
- We have two streams of thought-- our intellect and our God mind set.
- All great achievements begin with a burning desire!

Possibilities for your life

Everything you do as a believer, should be in the power of God. God wants to be a part of everything you do. Through God, you can do amazing things. All He asks that you do is to abide in Him, and He in you.

"With men this is impossible, but with God all things are possible."
—Matthew 19:26b

"In all your ways acknowledge Him and He shall direct your path."
—Proverbs 3:6

"The power which resides in man is new in nature, and none but he knows what is which he can do, nor does he know until he has tried."
—Ralph W. Emerson

"Within you right now is the power to do things you never dreamed possible. This power becomes available to you just as soon as you can change your beliefs."
— Maxwell Maltz

"There is always room at the top."
—Daniel Webster

"Everyone has a fair turn to be as great as he pleases."
—Jeremy Collier

"While there's life there's hope."
—Marcus Tullius Cicero

"Always be all that you can be and when you are all that you can be, it is enough."
—A.L. Williams

Thoughts to meditate upon to Prepare for God's Abundant Life:

- God gave you possibilities to be great. All you need is His daily direction in your life.

- If you can just dream it, you can be it.

- God gave us the ability to dream to introduce us to our higher self.

- As a child of God, you have the power to be whatever you dream available to you.

Taking action for your life

A great idea in the mind of anyone will not amount to anything, until you take action.

It is written:

"If you have faith as a mustard seed, you will say to this mountain, 'Move from here to there,' and it will move; and nothing will be impossible for you."
—Matthew 17:20

"The secret of getting things done is to act."
—Benjamin O. Davis

"Nothing comes by just thinking about it."
— John Wannamaker

When you get a great idea, you must act upon it, and not wait until all the necessary conditions are just right. Not all conditions will ever be right. People set goals to get things done and take action for a desired result. If you decide to wait for all conditions to be perfect, you will wait forever.

It is not hard to get into the action habit. It is a matter of a think-action mindset. You can train yourself to be a self-starter by using an affirmation like, "I will start this project now. I will not allow anyone or anything to postpone the action needed to begin this project." Say to yourself, "I need to take action to get results. I will not get results until I act."

Remember this; nothing is done without taking action. Look around you and observe the objects in your environment. Everything you see was once an idea or thought that was acted on. When you have an idea, you always have a choice. You can choose to be active and get results, or choose to be passive and get nothing.

If you have a vision, start at once to put something in action to get your vision on the way. Starting with some small chore will give you some positive feedback that your vision is attainable.

"A journey of a thousand miles begins with the first step."
— Chinese Proverb

Once you begin to take action, expect some future obstacles and difficulties. Any venture presents some risks, problems, or uncertainties. This is only life testing you to see if you are worthy of realizing your vision. This price tag must be paid to reach your dream. So pay the price to get what you want.

Remember, winners will always be willing to pay the cost of success. The losers' mentality, believes that there is a free lunch. Losers are not willing to pay the price for success. That is why they are quitters.

Losers never win, and winners never quit. It is not in the winners' vocabulary to quit. As believers, you should always be prepared to be a winner—to take action on your dreams. If you pause too long to deliberate, it will cost you something, such as loss of time, and prolonging the attainment of your goal.

As a believer, and a winner, never put off until tomorrow what you can do today. Be a crusader; know that God's assignment may be for you to lead the crowd. Know that God will be with you along the way.

THOUGHTS TO MEDITATE UPON
TO PREPARE FOR GOD'S ABUNDANT LIFE:

- Set a time to take action.
- Our goals are a series of actions. When we act, we create the momentum that is necessary to reach our goal.
- Start each day with God. When you follow His direction, success is assured.
- Ask God throughout your work day to give you godly thoughts, consequently you will take godly actions.

2

YOUR VISION FOR WEALTH

*"Write the vision and make it plain on tablets,
that He may run who reads it."*

—HABAKKUK 2:2

When God wants something big to happen on this earth, He plants a vision or dream in the heart of His people. Once God puts the vision in us, it causes us to be stretched and challenged, just as He stretched and challenged the visions planted within Paul, Joseph, Abraham, Moses, and John the Baptist.

"Know thyself, believe in God, and dare to dream."
— JOHN SALLEY

When you have a vision or dream, you must first examine yourself and undergo a change—one of a renewed mind. You must be primed for God's work in pursuing any vision. We cannot accomplish a vision without the help of God. We must also be changed by God, to have the proper mindset for effectively realizing the vision. We must be molded, like clay, for God to use us.

IT IS WRITTEN:

"But now, O Lord, You are our Father; We are the clay, and You are our Potter; And all we are the work of Your hand."
—ISAIAH 64:8

God will give you a vision because He believes in you. He knows your potential. You will be able to see the possibilities to handle the vision only with God as your helper. Without God, you cannot realize the vision. God will encourage your pursuits, because He knows you will need the encouragement.

There will be times when things will be difficult, but you must never quit. Your vision will need the support of those who are part of the vision. This is where you will need God's help.

Why should you be thankful for your vision? Because in the absence of a vision, mediocrity and commonalty will prevail in your life. God wants you to be all that you can be. Because of this, you will be fruitful when God gets the glory for your achievements.

There is a price, however, that you will have to pay to accomplish your vision. "What is the price?" you ask. The price will be a willingness to sacrifice—giving up immediate pleasures, working long hours, greater time away from your family, etc.—in order to spend the necessary time to pursue your vision.

You must put off the enjoyment of life today, to reap the rewards later. Either you can pay to pursue your dreams now, and enjoy life tomorrow, or you can enjoy life today and pay the price in the future that may be void of enjoyment. Either way, you cannot avoid the price.

The happiest people in the world are those who are living out their vision. They are giving themselves the impetus to rise above the day to day cares of the world. Their visions are bigger than they are.

You can lose yourself in something that is bigger than you. Your vision can serve as a vital part in your happiness. A vision creates energy in its owner, and gives hope and meaning to one's life.

You must put all of your energy and effort toward your dream. Be willing to pay the price—sacrifice that which God asks. Know that you will be rewarded at the time He deems it right.

God knows what it will take to achieve your dreams. He is there to help. Be on the lookout for God to send help your way in the form of instructions, hints, ideas, and through people. God wants you to win so that He can get the glory for your achievement. After all, you are His child and one of His trophies. Always remember, you are working within the strength of Jesus Christ, your partner.

You must always exhibit an attitude of confidence in the company of others. But remember that the source of your confidence is in the Lord, who lives inside of you. As a result, you will begin to grow in confidence inwardly. The way we act outwardly affects how we are inwardly.

Make sure you explore every possible avenue to reach your dream. Do not let any dead end street or detour stop you. Find another way to proceed with your dream.

Everyone needs a dream. God made us that way. We are goal-oriented beings. Dreams and visions prevent us from drifting in life. They give us a sense of balance and direction.

Imagine a sailboat at sea without a captain to set its sail. This boat could end up anywhere with a shift in wind direction. Now, place a captain at the helm of the boat with a goal to sail toward London, England. In time, the boat will arrive at the shores of London, England because there was a captain at the helm with a goal.

Just as the boat will arrive in London with a captain at the helm, our goals will be attained when we take the helm. We must have goals and dreams to give our lives meaning and to prevent us from drifting.

You have been given a mind of "possibility thinking" by God himself. Your vision is the key that opens the door to your destiny. Success is your birthright.

"Some people dream of great accomplishments, while others stay awake and do them."

—CONSTANCE NEWMAN

THOUGHTS TO MEDITATE UPON TO PREPARE FOR GOD'S ABUNDANT LIFE:

- Write the vision.
- Make plans.
- Get the cooperation of others.
- Take action.
- Pursue the vision with prayer, vigor, hope, and faith.

Always have an "I can" attitude

Simply having a vision alone, however, is not enough. It must be combined with venture and courage.

IT IS WRITTEN:

"I can do all things through Christ who strengthens me."

—PHILIPPIANS 4:13

Let me remind you, God gave you a "can do" mind. You will always accomplish more in life by having an "I can" attitude. When you think "I can" instead of "I can't," you tend to get what you think.

"If you think you can, or if you think you can't, either way — you are right."

—HENRY FORD

Think of how much more of a positive impact you could have on your life and the lives of others, if only you would adopt an "I can" attitude. There are so many things in life that are contingent upon your attitude. You make many choices daily, and your decisions are based largely on your attitude.

Having the right attitude can make you, and having the wrong attitude can break you. It is just that simple. It is often stated that "attitude will largely determine your altitude, and not our education."

This poem says it best:

If you think you are beaten, you are
If you think you dare not, You don't
If you like to win, but think you can't
It is almost certain you won't
If you think you'll lose, you've lost
For out of the world we find
Success begins with a fellow's will
It's all in the state of mind
If you think you are out classed, you are
You got to think high to rise
You got to be sure of yourself before
You can ever win a prize
Life's battles don't always go to
The stronger or faster man
But sooner or later, the man who wins
Is the man who thinks He can
                    —Author Unknown (Unknown n.d.)

Having the right attitude is a simple process of thought management. You must learn to manage your thoughts at all times to have the right attitude at all times.

You can adopt an "I can" attitude by managing your thoughts. You should think "I can" until this thought is well embedded in your hearts, and your subconscious mind.

It is written:

"As a man thinks in his heart, so is He."
—Proverbs 23:7

Most people live too far beneath their "God-given" power. If you truly focus on all the attributes that God has given you, you would feel happier, stronger, and more alive; be more wonderful, more active, more successful, a lot more faithful, and spiritual; and finally—a lot more "God like."

Thoughts to meditate upon
to Prepare for God's Abundant Life:

- Your attitude should be "I can do all things when God strengthens me."
- The believer can do anything he can imagine.
- The believer's life should be centered around "I can be anything I desire to be."

Programming your mind to win

God gave you a mind that responds to autosuggestion and programming. Because God gave you a subconscious, you can form good and bad habits. Everything that has happened to you is stored in the subconscious. All decisions you make come from the subconscious level of your mind.

In a way, your mind is like a computer. It stores information. You can read and absorb enough positive information from a self-help book or the Bible to program your mind to win in life.

Reading the Bible often will give you the confidence to believe what God says about you. God's view of every believer is positive and uplifting. To be fully successful, you must know the truth about God living on the inside of you.

The Bible tells us that we are to "imitate" God. We are made in the image of God. Everything that God created was a success. The Bible is a success manual. Every success book has some principles that come from the Bible. A believer can become successful by studying, believing, and doing God's Word.

The principles in the Bible are God's way of directing His children toward success. God wants the best for His children. God desires success for His children more than His children desire success for themselves.

The Bible is saturated with all the help a believer needs to attain success in any field of endeavor. God said in His Word that He would always be with His children. He also said that He would not forsake His children.

All you need, as a believer, is God and His Word to achieve anything in life that is the will of the Father. God also desires for His children to be number one, not number two, or number three. It is God who gets the glory when each of His children comes in first place in a contest. When you feed from the Word of God daily, you are programming your mind to be all that God intended for you to be.

God has made many promises in the Bible for His children. These promises are for us to live by and have the things in life that are pleasing to Him.

Thoughts to meditate upon to Prepare for God's Abundant Life:

- In everything you do, think "win," because you are a believer, a child of Almighty God.
- As you think "win," your heart and spirit should be saying, "I will win because God is with me."
- Thinking "win," should become a habit with you.
- When you think in terms of winning, the "how to win" will follow. Just act on it.

3

ACHIEVING EXCELLENCE FOR WEALTH

*"I will praise You, for I am fearfully and
wonderfully made; Marvelous are Your works, And
that my soul knows very well."*

—PSALM 139:14

Excellence means going far beyond the call of duty, and doing more than others expect. It comes from striving, maintaining the highest standards, and looking after the smallest detail.

Stop for a moment and consider the fact that you were made in the "Image of Almighty God," the "Creator of the Universe."

It is written:

"Then God said, 'Let Us make man in Our image,
according to Our likeness."
—Genesis 1:26

There is no other creature God made that can compare to the human species. We were made by God to do great things in life for His glory!

It is written:

"Most assuredly, I say to you, he who believes in Me,
the works that I do he will do also; and greater works than
these he will do, because I go to my Father."
—John 14:12

Whatever you do, get better at it every day. You honor God when you do your very best. Your attitude should be, "I will glorify God by doing my best."

I believe that God put a "seed of greatness" in man; something that He did not put in any other creature He made. There is no other blueprint quite like the blueprint of man. When God created man, His blueprint was never intended for use again.

God has allowed man to do great and marvelous things. Man has been able to travel to the moon, and explore the universe with advanced technology and aerospace engineering. God has allowed man to master medical achievements never imagined before.

Each of you has a "seed of greatness" that has been planted in you by God. Yet, there are still few who fully recognize their potential. Only God is aware of man's full potential.

Your imagination alone can allow you to create inventions and travel to foreign places, even without leaving your living room. God gave you a subconscious mind that contains all the information that you have ever seen, heard, tasted, or felt. I believe your memory system is capable of holding more information than many computers. This is how God made you. You are "fearfully and wonderfully made."

Man can do anything imaginable. Man's imagination is powerful. There is no limit to the imagination of man. The Bible also says we are "gods."

IT IS WRITTEN:

"I said, 'You are "gods"; And all of you are children of the Most High."

—PSALM 82:6

Without God, it is impossible for man to use all of his potential fully. Because the power of God is within us, we should always strive for excellence in everything we do. Each one of us has the potential to contribute something to the earth. We can make the world a better place to live by using our God given talents to affect this planet.

Many inventions are not yet made. These inventions are still in the minds of men, just waiting to be birthed and developed. The power of thought comes from God himself. Everything that you can see that was made by man was a thought in the mind of man.

Just imagine all the things that God created in the universe. When I look at the sun, stars, planets and the moon, the first thing that comes to mind is perfection, excellence and thoughts that at one time, were in the mind of God.

You can do great things also, when you have a close relationship with God. When you focus on God, there are no limits to what you can do. God has placed power within you. You only need to believe and have faith in God.

You must constantly study to improve yourselves. If you work to get better, God is honored and He will favor your efforts. You should always do more than what is required of you. This brings God into the picture.

IT IS WRITTEN:

"In all the work you are doing, work the best you can,
work as if you were doing it for the Lord, not for people."
—COLOSSIANS 3:23

In other words, strive for "excellence" in everything you do. Average is not good enough. It is said that average is best of the worst and worst of the best.

Remember, if something is worth doing, it is worth doing well. Think "excellence" in everything you do.

God did not make average human beings. People make themselves average by thinking average and then performing average. Model your thinking, actions, and behavior after the best. Keep moving toward "excellence" and enjoy the rewards.

"Excellence is to do a common thing in an uncommon way."
— BOOKER T. WASHINGTON

There are no prizes for average performances. Therefore, do not undertake that which you cannot do in an excellent fashion.

THOUGHTS TO MEDITATE UPON
TO PREPARE FOR GOD'S ABUNDANT LIFE:

- Decide today that you will maximize your potential to honor God.
- Consider this—God displayed excellence in all that He did.
- God said for us to imitate Him.
- Think of ways you can do what you do even better.

What God thinks of His children

IT IS WRITTEN:

"There is now no condemnation to those who are in Christ Jesus, who do not walk according to the flesh, but according to the Spirit."
—ROMANS 8:1

"Being justified freely by His grace through the redemption that is in Christ Jesus, Whom God presented Him as a sacrifice of atonement."
—ROMANS 3:24

This atonement means that through the blood of Jesus Christ, God has declared all believers as righteous.

IT IS WRITTEN:

Now, therefore, you are no longer strangers and foreigners, but fellow citizens with the saints and members of the household of God.
—EPHESIANS 2:19

Just as you have brothers and sisters in your own household, you have many brothers and sisters in the household of God. Every believer is a member of God's family. He has a large family and a place for you to belong.

Because of Jesus' sacrifice for our sins, we as believers received the benefit of being cleansed, as though we had never sinned. When God looks at us, He sees the "righteousness of Jesus."

IT IS WRITTEN:

*"For I will forgive their iniquity, and their sin I will
remember no more."*
—JEREMIAH 31:34

Now do you understand how God sees His children? We do not
have to feel guilty about our past sins anymore. We have been completely
forgiven, because of what Jesus did on the cross. We are God's chosen
people. We are in the family of God, and He sees us as His dear children.
We should think this way about ourselves.

THOUGHTS TO MEDITATE UPON
TO PREPARE FOR GOD'S ABUNDANT LIFE:

- See yourself as a righteous believer because of the shed
  blood of Jesus Christ.

- As a believer, God sees you as guiltless, and sinless.

- You have been chosen by God. Every believer was selected
  by God.

- God sees you as His special child.

The right attitude for life

The believer's attitude is influenced by the Word of God. It is our mindset that will determine our attitude.

IT IS WRITTEN:

"Who has known the mind of the Lord that He may instruct Him? But we have the mind of Christ."
—1 CORINTHIANS 2:16

As we abide in God, and His Word abides in us, we have the mind of Christ. Therefore, we should respond to any circumstance with a Christ-like Spirit.

IT IS WRITTEN:

"Let the word of Christ dwell in you richly in all wisdom, teaching and admonishing one another in psalms and hymns and spiritual songs, singing with grace in your hearts to the Lord."
—COLOSSIANS 3:16

In any circumstance, we can choose to respond positively or negatively. It is how we react to events that demonstrates our attitude, and not the events themselves. God's Word should always guide our attitude, rather than our circumstances. God is advancing the believer's life to be more like the life of Christ.

"It is not the situation. It is your reaction to the situation."
—BOB CONKLIN

"Your living is determined not so much by what life brings to you as by the attitude you bring to life; not so much by what happens to you as by the way your mind looks at what happens."
—JOHN HOMER MILLER

"No one on earth can hurt you, unless you accept the hurt in your own mind...The problem is not other people; it is your reaction."
—VERNON HOWARD

"Life at anytime can become difficult: life at anytime can become easy. It all depends upon how one adjusts oneself to life."
—MORARJI DESAI

"Any fact facing us is not as important as our attitude towards it, for that determines our success or failure."
—NORMAN VINCENT PEALE

THOUGHTS TO MEDITATE UPON TO PREPARE FOR GOD'S ABUNDANT LIFE:

- Attitude is a choice. If the believer is abiding in God's Word, his attitude should be "Christ-like."

- God's Word should determine the believers' attitude and not circumstances.

- Adopt the attitude that God placed you on this earth for a purpose.

Why God created you in His image

IT IS WRITTEN:

"Then God said, 'Let Us make man in Our image, according to Our likeness; let them have dominion over the fish of the sea, over the birds of the air, over the cattle, over all the earth and over every creeping thing that creeps on the earth."

—GENESIS 1:26

Here are several reasons God may have created us in His own image.

- God wanted man to reflect His nature.
- God wanted to fellowship with man.
- God wanted man to have dominion over the earth.
- God wanted earthly children, as He told Adam and Eve to be fruitful and multiply.

God in essence assigned men to be small gods on the earth. We are indeed little gods according to Scripture.

IT IS WRITTEN:

"I said, 'You are gods.' And all of you are all children of the Most High."

—PSALM 82:6

THOUGHTS TO MEDITATE UPON
TO PREPARE FOR GOD'S ABUNDANT LIFE:

- Remember, we were created in God's Image.
- God instructed us to imitate Him.
- God said, "we shall have what we say."
- Our words have power. Use them for God's glory.

4

ooooo

WEALTH AND LOVING OTHERS

"Love the Lord your God with all your heart, all your soul, all your mind and all your strength. The second command is this: Love your neighbor as you love yourself. There is no commandment greater than these."

—MARK 12:30-31

Develop an "attitude of gratitude." Say thanks to everyone you meet for everything they do for you. Love and never criticize, condemn or complain in a conversation with others. Speak well of others and look for something good to say.

The test of love is expressed in the three "C's" of leadership: caring, consideration and courtesy. The kindest thing you can do for the people you love and care about is to become a happy, joyous person.

Happiness comes when you believe in what you are doing, know what you are doing, and love what you are doing. Love only grows by sharing. You will receive more love, when you give and share love with others. Focus on giving love without expecting anything in return.

IT IS WRITTEN:

"And now abide faith, hope, love, these three; but the greatest of these is love."

—1 CORINTHIANS 13:13

By loving God and others, every one of God's rules is fulfilled. Loving God with everything you are—with all your emotions, intellect, and energy—is what gives you the desire and wisdom you need to love others well. Anytime you are in doubt as to what God wants you to do in a given situation, ask yourself "Right now, how can I love God and others best?"

IT IS WRITTEN:

"If I give all I possess to the poor and surrender my body to the flames, but have not love, I gain nothing. Love is patient, love is kind. It does not envy, it does not boast, it is not proud."

—1 CORINTHIANS 13:3-4(NIV)

"This is my commandment, that you love one another
as I have loved you."
—JOHN 15:12

Without giving love, you have no seed that will prosper. The Bible tells you that giving and helping the poor is of no profit, if there is no love in your heart.

IT IS WRITTEN:

"And though I bestow all of my goods to feed the poor,
and though I give my body to be burned, but have not
love, it profits me nothing."
—1 CORINTHIANS 13:3

How do we know that God abides in us? When we love one another, "we know that God abides in us, and His love has been perfected in us." (1 John 4:12) Conversely, when we hate our brother, we do not love God!

IT IS WRITTEN:

"If someone says, I love God and hates his brother,
He is a liar, for He who does not love his brother whom He
has seen, how can He love God Whom He has not seen?"
—1 JOHN 4:20

We should love God for Who He is and also because He first loved us. Surely, if we love God, we must also love our brother.

Thoughts to meditate upon
to Prepare for God's Abundant Life:

- Our love for others is the second greatest commandment.
- If we can't love one another, who we can see; how can we love God, Who we cannot see?
- Love God with all your mind, soul and strength.
- We are commanded by God to love our neighbor.

Pride and humility

The Lord refuses to share "His glory" with anyone! When we say, "Look at what I have accomplished, look at me, or look at who I am," we take all of "God's glory" for ourselves! God hates it! Any good in us is by God's design. We have no goodness in us apart from God's goodness in us.

Pride in the form of conceit, arrogance, vanity, or pomposity always ends in destruction—and we usually end up losing those things we are boastful or proud of. We must never seek to take "God's glory" for ourselves. Misplaced pride makes us useless for the kingdom of God!

Anything and everything that we have, God enabled us to get it. Apart from God, we cannot get anything on our own. God must empower us.

IT IS WRITTEN:

"The Lord lifts up the humble; He casts the wicked down to the ground."

—Psalm 147:6

In everything that we do, we must be careful not to be proud or boastful. God applauds a humble spirit. We do not ever want God to resist us.

IT IS WRITTEN:

"God resists the proud, but gives grace to the humble."
—1 Peter 5:5

"Therefore, humble yourselves under the mighty hand of God, that He may exalt you in due time."
—1 Peter 5:6

41

Why does God hate pride so much? Human feelings, attitudes, and demonstrations of arrogance, conceit, smugness, and self-importance, interfere with God's ability to use us for His purpose. You might say that God puts pride and murder in the same category.

Arrogant people believe they can succeed in life solely by their own strength. Arrogant behavior is a demonstration of pride. The most destructive thing about pride is that it pushes God away from the center of your life. Now you are in disobedience with God's Word.

God hates a proud look. God originally made the Devil a beautiful angel. The Devil became proud of his beauty and He wanted God's position in heaven. So God kicked Satan out of heaven and one third of the angels left heaven with the Devil. The Devil and all of his fallen angels are here on the earth to do the work of the Devil, that is "to steal, kill, and destroy."(John 10:10).

IT IS WRITTEN:

"Pride goes before destruction, and a haughty spirit before a fall."

—PROVERBS 16:18

While success is what every child of God is seeking, we cannot accomplish anything apart from God. Without Him, we would not have any power, strength, or faith to do anything. We are hopeless without Him.

When we accomplish something, whether it is small or large, we should always give God the credit. In this way, God gets the glory. After all, He made us and He equipped us with gifts and talents to accomplish His plan and purpose for our lives.

God will lift us up and reward us in many wonderful ways when we are humble. He will not bless a proud or haughty spirit. God will resist the proud and He will bless the humble.

IT IS WRITTEN:

"Great is the Lord and mighty in power; His understanding is infinite."

—PSALM 147:5

Remember, God is love, and we must walk in a humble way before Him at all times under all circumstances. If we exalt ourselves, God will humble us. God rules over all. We are to be submissive to Him and never show any form of pride.

It is good to want to do great things. However, it must be for the right reason—to bring "glory to God," not yourself.

THOUGHTS TO MEDITATE UPON
TO PREPARE FOR GOD'S ABUNDANT LIFE:

- Acknowledge God in all your ways and He will direct your path.
- Tell God you need Him daily, and you cannot do anything without Him.
- Stay focused on God to have power in your life.
- Give God the glory for all your accomplishments.
- Focus on how you can help others, so that pride will not take root in your life.

A "God" mindset

Throughout the developed world, we have moved from "man power" to "mind power!" We have moved from the use of physical muscles to the use of mental muscles, and all its forces that will determine our future.

At midnight on May 17, 2009, I felt God speak to my heart that all of His children are winners, but they are not aware of it; because they do not have a "God" mindset. God said that He is the Almighty God. His children have the attributes of the Father. God's children can also do the mighty things of God if they keep a "God" mindset and live a holy life.

When I received this revelation from God, my whole life took on a new meaning. I understood that I could do the things God can do if I maintain a "God consciousness;" I have power to achieve whatever I desire in life. I am a winner because God is the Chief Winner. He said no one could stand up against Him.

God has the victory in everything. As His offspring, we can also have victory in everything. We may not attain our victory at first because we must undergo a learning process. Having faith is a learning process, just as winning is a learning process.

God wants us to think as winners, because He said to imitate Him. I know it is better to approach any challenge in life with a "God" mindset than to approach a challenge without a "God" mindset. When we operate with a "God" mindset, we attract "power energy" from within. This energy is God's energy and it is powerful. It is so powerful it baffles the imagination. However, it only comes through belief, faith, and continual practice. This is a patient process.

I believe that non-believers can use this energy without being aware of it. It is present in the universe. However, this power is intended for God's children to use. But, there must be a strong sense of belief in one's ability coupled with a "God" consciousness.

We are like God in many aspects. He gave us this power for us to operate on this earth. God handed over to man, the "power" to dominate the whole earth.

It is written:

"Then God said, 'Let us make man in Our image, according to Our likeness; let them have dominion over the fish of the sea, over the birds of the air, and over the cattle, over all the earth and over every creeping thing that creeps on the earth."

—Genesis 1:26

I truly believe that God in His infinite wisdom gave us the power to dominate the whole earth, but also to have dominion over our circumstances.

It occurred to me that our circumstances, problems, and challenges are a part of this earth. Consequently, we have dominion over all of them with a "God consciousness." Having a "God" mindset does not mean that you can do these things without God. But, you can do these things in the "power of God."

It is written:

"I can do all things through Christ Who strengthens me."

—Philippians 4:13

Man, in himself without God, is weak. He becomes strong only after he realizes who he is in Christ, and when he is fully aware of what God says about him.

Once our thoughts line up with God's thoughts, we become like a living dynamo. This is how God made us, but the power that God placed inside of us is underdeveloped. This "God" power can only be tapped into in its entirety by having a personal relationship with Jesus Christ.

Our thoughts come from our mind, and turn into visible manifestations. We have the "mind of Christ" to create what we desire in life.

IT IS WRITTEN:

"For who knows the mind of the Lord that He may instruct him? But we have the mind of Christ."
—1 CORINTHIANS 2:16

Remember, when we hold God in the "Highest Esteem," as the One who is in authority over us, we are winners. When we are "God conscious" and imitate God; we stimulate a higher performance in everything we do.

We must never forget that the power that God gives us can never be interpreted as power outside of God's grace. Without God, we have no power. In fact, we are weak, but with Him, we are strong. We are operating in God's power in the correct way.

God insists that even when we have power in His strength, we must remain humble. We can never exalt ourselves. God will not allow it.

THOUGHTS TO MEDITATE UPON
TO PREPARE FOR GOD'S ABUNDANT LIFE:

- Most of our awakened day should be focused on God.
- Peace is a result of a "God" mind-set.
- There is power in a "God" mind-set.
- Faith is a result of a "God" mind-set.

46

5

ooooo

POWER AND WEALTH

"The God of Israel is He who gives strength and power to His people."

—PSALM 68:35B

God has given each believer a measure of power to; speak, run, talk, work, sing, think, etc. Never take this power for granted! It is God's gift to you!

The power that God gives to His children must be activated and used constantly. If there is no awareness of this power, it is of no use to the believer. Also, if this power is not used it will be lost.

Power comes from knowing that you have power to do something. People with power are people who are aware of how to get things done. When we educate ourselves, we build power to accomplish our goals.

There is power in prayer. God will always give us power to accomplish what we need to accomplish. A burning desire will always bring power to the person with the desire. If we fail to get knowledge, we will not have the power we need. Being without knowledge is being without power.

The believer can get power from ideas, thoughts, knowledge, desires, visions, goals, dreams, prayers, understanding, information or beliefs:

"Every thought you entertain is power that goes out, and every thought comes back laden with its kind."
—Ralph Waldo Trent

Every believer that relies totally on God through prayer and faith has all the power he needs. However, he must develop and use it for the good of God's kingdom and others. When the believer chooses to believe, he is endued with power. Faith begets power from God. When we rely on God through faith, He acts on our behalf.

As believers, we must know that the more of God's Word we put into our hearts, the greater the power we have. We all need God daily. When we say aloud, "Jesus is Lord," we affirm our belief in the power of God. Remember, our words have power!

- Every believer has power given to him from God.
- Every believer has some of the attributes of God.
- God made us to be like Him in some ways.
- The believer can speak to his mountain.

In Christ you can do great things

It is written:

*"Yet it shall not be so among you; but whoever desires
to become great among you, let him be your servant."*
—Matthew 20:26

Every study of high achieving men and women proves that greatness in life is only possible after you become outstanding, not only in your chosen field, but in life. They identified their visions and dreams, adequately prepared for the pursuit of their dreams, developed plans to accomplish their goals, and passionately pursued them.

Those who have attained greatness paid the price of constant struggle, setbacks, battles, and disappointments. Throughout life, they learned from their mistakes, faced their fears, overcame their weaknesses, utilized their strengths, and never gave up.

One other observation about extremely successful people—whether public or private sector leaders, politicians, civic leaders, scientists, educators, physicians, entertainers, etc.—is their ongoing desire and commitment to "make the world a better place" through contributions and personal involvement. Through their own faith and belief systems, they are fully aware of their obligation to give back to their communities, to society, and the world-at-large for the blessings they have received.

They paid the price, made the sacrifices, gave back to the world, and became the best in their field. They have been richly rewarded.

The Bible tells us to study to show ourselves approved. If you would read an hour per day in your chosen field, this would work out to be about one book per week; fifty per year and will lead you to success. Learn what you need to learn and practice it until you become proficient.

The great secret of success is that there are no secrets of success. Success comes when you do what you love to do and commit to being the best in your field.

Strive to make yourself invaluable in your vocation, to your family, to your church, and to God to the point of being indispensable. Your success in business, as well as your family and personal life will be in direct proportion to what you do after you have done what you are expected to do.

"Try not to become a man of success but rather try to become a man of value."
—Albert Einstein

Make up your mind to succeed and persist until you do, no matter what the difficulties dictate. Always remember to ask and rely on God to direct your steps!

You can be great! But, remember your success is not measured simply by the value of monetary wealth, but by value of your total life to others and to God.

- Every great success is an accumulation of thousands of ordinary efforts that no one sees or appreciates.

- Your outer world of success, achievements, and relationships will always be a reflection of your inner attitudes of mind.

- Focus on God's Word that tells us: "With God all things are possible." (Matthew 10:26)

- The Bible tells us that we can do all things through Christ who strengthens us." (Philippians 4:13)

God has an assignment for you

Just as God had assignments for different people in the Scriptures, He also has an assignment for you. God will not give you an assignment that He did not give you the ability to carry out. The clue to your assignment are those things you are good at doing, and the things you enjoy doing—usually your God-given talents.

IT IS WRITTEN:

"Before I formed you in the womb I knew you, before you were born I set you apart."

— JEREMIAH 1:5(NIV)

"For we are His workmanship, created in Christ Jesus for good works, which God prepared beforehand that we should walk in them."

— EPHESIANS 2:10

Everything that you have on the inside of you, God gave to you. God had a purpose in giving you these inborn interests. Never ignore your interest. Consider how they might be used for God's glory. There is a distinct reason why you love to do certain things.

Remember that we are commanded to serve God, just like Jesus was commanded to serve others.

It is written:

"Just as the Son of Man did not come to be served but to serve, and to give His life as a ransom for many."
—MATTHEW 20:28(NIV)

For believers, service is not optional. At the heart of the believers' life is the desire to serve and to give.

"Holy living consists in doing God's work with a smile."
—MOTHER TERESA

The last thing believers need to do is attend another Bible study. You already know enough to start serving God. As believers, you must act on what you know, and practice what you claim to believe.

What is needed is serving experience. You must exercise your spiritual muscles. Believers should be asking themselves, "whose needs can I meet?"

Remember, we will all ultimately stand before God to be evaluated on how well we served others.

"Serve the Lord with all your heart for you, brethren, have been called to liberty; only do not use liberty as an opportunity for the flesh, but through love serve one another."

—GALATIANS 5:13

We should not just settle for the good life because the good life is not good enough. It is not fulfilling. The richest man in the world once said, "A simple life in the fear of God is better than a rich life with a ton of headaches." (Proverbs 15:16)

Go to God in prayer and ask Him to help you know your assignment. God will be happy to reveal the answer.

THOUGHTS TO MEDITATE UPON
TO PREPARE FOR GOD'S ABUNDANT LIFE:

- We are to seek God to discover our assignment on earth.
- Whatever our assignment is, it will be fulfilling.
- Our assignment makes us complete.

Know what you want and you will get it

One of the main reasons that most believers do not accomplish much in life is because they have a tough time making up their minds about what they want. Today, there are so many options and so many choices that the average person just can't make a definite decision about what to do. They try so many things looking for what may give them passion and fulfillment, but if a person doesn't have a definite purpose in life, it is almost impossible to get excited about life itself. The believer has the right to seek God for help in this area.

God has given every person gifts and talents to fulfill the purpose that God has assigned to him. Remember God has the answer to every believers problem. God made us and He knows what is best for us. We must admit that we need His help in many ways. Lack of confidence will sometimes keep the believer from pursuing a dream that is in his heart. We must realize that Jesus is our confidence, and Jesus is our life and hope. We have to constantly remind ourselves that with Jesus, there is nothing we can't do. The more we learn about God, the better we will know Him, and the better we know Him, the greater our confidence should increase. Why? Because He is in our hearts and thoughts. This also means that God is operating in our lives to mature us and reveal more of Himself to us. We are powerful and conquerors in the eyes of God. God sees us in a different way than we see ourselves. We may have some weak areas in our lives, but the power of God makes up for the weak areas through His grace. We need to recognize that there is no weakness in God. There is love and power in God that we can draw upon at anytime to do the things we should do. It is all available to us just for the asking. The Bible tells us that we have not, because we ask not.

Remember, it is your passion and purpose in life that gives energy. Your purpose gives value to your life. If we are working at something, and we don't get excitement and energy, we may not be operating in our purpose. Our purpose should be life fulfilling and make us complete.

Thoughts to meditate upon
to Prepare for God's Abundant Life:

- Seek God to help you discover your purpose.
- Remember that God has a planned purpose for every believer.
- Put your purpose in writing. Review it often.
- Ask God to strengthen you to gain the confidence to pursue your purpose

6

Waiting on God for Wealth

"The Lord is good to those who wait for Him, to the soul who seeks Him."

—Lamentations 3:25

We live in a "now" generation, where our priorities are reflected through our wants, desires, and acquisitions are based upon the need for immediate gratification. Television and radio programming, along with every other form of advertising influence our decisions to acquire that which provides a perceived lifestyle of comfort and status. We are even provided insight into opportunities that enable us to avail ourselves of material items, that otherwise are not affordable for us now. We are persuaded that we can have what we want now.

The influx of "fast-food" restaurants has spurned entire business segments with "easy access, fast, quick, no waiting, etc." as their primary competitive edge. We have been so conditioned to believe that waiting is not necessary, and that to do so is a sign of poor or lack luster business practices or customer service.

When we find ourselves having to wait, we do so impatiently—often demonstrating our disgruntled feelings through emotional outbursts, irrational decisions, other disruptive behaviors, and a lack of compassion or empathy towards another. All of which, are contrary to one's belief, faith, and trust in God.

God wants you to demonstrate patience—the capacity for waiting: the ability to endure waiting, delay, or provocation without becoming annoyed or upset, or to persevere calmly when faced with difficulties (Microsoft Corporation 2009) In fact, God will sometimes delay a promise to teach you patience and faith. When you patiently wait, God promises to reward you.

IT IS WRITTEN:

"They shall not be ashamed who wait for me."
— ISAIAH 49:23

Isaiah spoke of the God, "Who acts for the one who waits for Him."
—ISAIAH 64:4

God will often make the believer wait. The reason for the wait lies with God himself. For God is the "Master" trainer. He knows the heart of man, and what he needs. You must remember however, that while you actively wait, God actively works on your behalf.

"Everything comes if a man will only wait."
—BENJAMIN DISRAELI

Waiting can be one of the most difficult things in the believer's life. But it is not wasted time at all. If you are sensitive to God's still, small voice, you will hear His instructions throughout your periods of waiting. He may even change your circumstances, while you wait on Him. God uses the time of waiting to shift your motives and strengthen your faith.

IT IS WRITTEN:

"Wait on the Lord; be of good courage, and He shall strengthen your heart; wait, I say, on the Lord!"
—PSALM 27:14

Know that when you have waited on Him patiently and faithfully, God will reward you with blessings, both large and unexpected. Remember, God acts on behalf of those who wait for Him.

IT IS WRITTEN:

"Those who wait on the Lord, shall inherit the earth."
—PSALM 37:9

"Rest in the Lord, and wait patiently for Him; Do not fret because of Him who prospers in his way."
—PSALM 37:7

Why does God make you wait? God wants you to submit to His will, to depend on Him and not on yourself or others. God also wants to teach you to trust His ways and timing, and learn that His ways are better than your ways. He wants to teach discipline and obedience to you. What is more, God wants you to stop and listen to His voice, especially when your impatience reflects upon actions, deeds, or thoughts that are not pleasing to Him.

While going through difficult times, we learn to endure, to persevere, and to hold on even when there is no help in sight. The Bible is filled with stories of followers who waited patiently on God and were blessed—Joseph, Abraham, David, Noah, Daniel, the three Hebrew children, Moses, Job, and Josiah.

God will teach you patience by making you wait. Through trials and tribulations, you will learn patience (James 1:2, Romans 5:3).

IT IS WRITTEN:

"Count it all joy, when we face trying times."
—JAMES 1:2

God will train the believer to wait on Him. Waiting is trusting. It honors God when His children wait patiently for Him. Waiting tests the heart and soul of man. God's love is always waiting when there is no answer or clue.

God knows all and He will not disappoint His children. Put your trust in God and wait on Him. The Bible says He will never leave or forsake those who believe in Him. God delights in giving His children the desires (promises) of their hearts.

Therefore, wait on Him!

Thoughts to meditate upon
to Prepare for God's Abundant Life:

- Wait on God, with the faith, belief, and understanding that everything is centered on His timing, not ours.

- God has a season that He has prepared just for you. Wait on Him.

- God has a specific reason for making you wait, if you but listen.

- Waiting requires faith and trust.

Meditation

Meditation is the "emptying of the mind of thoughts, or the concentration of the mind on one thing, in order to aid mental or spiritual development, contemplation, or relaxation." (Microsoft Corporation 2009) To ensure that you are making the right decisions, gaining spiritual guidance, and formalizing your visions, it is important to take time to quietly hear and visualize your thinking. Mediate upon your dreams every now and then.

See yourself enjoying your goal. Picture you in your dream as if it were real. If you do this often enough, your brain will accept this exercise as being real.

If it is your dream to own a business, see yourself in the everyday operation of the business. Picture your loved ones helping you with some of the functions of the business.

Your vision can become real in your imagination. Look at every detail of your dream and see the different characters and objects.

Confidence will come from meditation. You are seeing for yourself a sample of what your vision will be.

THOUGHTS TO MEDITATE UPON
TO PREPARE FOR GOD'S ABUNDANT LIFE:

- Meditation is silent focusing on something.
- To hold a single thought on an object in silence, is meditating.
- Meditating on God's Word will give us peace.

Problems are inevitable

For as long as we live, we will face problems in our lives. However, we can overcome the problems; not by our own strength, but because we have Jesus living inside of us.

It is written:

"My brethren, count it all joy when you fall into various trials, knowing that the testing of your faith produces patience. But let patience have its perfect work, that you may be perfect and complete, lacking nothing."
—James 1: 2-4

"In the world you will have tribulation; but be of good cheer, I have overcome the world."
—John 16:33

"You can always tell when you are on the road to success, it's uphill all the way. If you are not having any problems or difficulties, you are on a road that leads to nowhere."
—Paul Harvey

The wisest thing is to expect some problems and be ready for them. You can be ready by studying God's Word, so that you can stand on His promises. With understanding and faith, you have the ammunition needed to keep problems from blindsiding you.

Before every vision or dream is realized, there will always be some minor or major hurdles to climb over. This is a part of reality — the real world. The only place that a dream will happen without problems is in a fantasy world.

You must adopt an attitude of faith, that nothing will be able to stop you. You must have an unstoppable mindset and maintain an unstoppable mindset until you have reached your dream.

"I press toward the goal for the prize of the upward call of God in Christ Jesus."
—Philippians 3:14

God uses difficulties to make the believer strong. One tends to grow stronger through life's trials and tribulations, rather than from a life of ease and relaxation. God has a special mission for every believer, and God knows that faith is not enhanced unless tested through trials and tribulation. The believer knows that He can always depend on God for strength and encouragement.

Thoughts to meditate upon
to Prepare for God's Abundant Life:

- There will always be problems. Rely on prayer when they come.
- Fix your eyes on Jesus. He has overcome the world.
- Trust in the Lord when a problem arises. Acknowledge Him in all your ways, and He will direct you.

Satan— the enemy of getting wealth God's way

The Devil is a fallen angel and an enemy of God. He was kicked out of heaven because He lusted after God's position as the Supreme Creator. The Devil is a liar, thief and an enemy of all of God's children. And now, the Devil has set up his false kingdom here on earth.

It is written:

"The thief does not come except to steal, and to kill and to destroy."

—John 10:10a

The Devil is the god of this world. His mission is to keep unbelievers from the saving grace of Jesus Christ, consequently, destroying them. The Devil is not alone—one third of the angels in heaven decided to join ranks with the Devil here on earth.

Believers should not fear Satan because of Who lives within us. The Bible tells us that the Holy Spirit is within us.

It is written:

"He Who is in you is greater than He who is in the world."

—1 John 4:4

The Bible tells us, "The Devil, who deceived them, was cast into the lake of fire and brimstone where the beast and false prophet are. And they will be tormented day and night forever and ever."(Revelation 20:10). On earth, the Devil also condemns and attempts to fill the believer with fear, doubt and despair. His mission is to prevent the believer from praising and honoring God, which denies the believer of all of God's promises.

The Bible says that Satan is the ruler of the world, where we can be harassed, tempted or caused to make mistakes; mistakes that can lead us away from God. Yet the believer can still claim victory because of what Jesus did on the cross. He defeated sin on the cross once and for all! The Bible tells us that if we resist the Devil, he will flee from us.

Thoughts to meditate upon to Prepare for God's Abundant Life:

- Satan does not want you to pursue your vision — resist him and take the first step to attain your vision.
- Think big and set goals to make your vision a reality. Satan wants you to fail to spite God.
- Satan is in competition with God for your life!
- When you make God first place in your life, Satan is defeated. You are a winner in Christ but Satan will continue to harass you. Confess and stand on God's Word, for as long as you follow God, Satan will never stop.
- Remember, greater is He who is in you, than He that is in the world.

7

ooooo

COMMITMENT AND WEALTH

"Be steadfast, immovable, always abounding in the work of the Lord, knowing that your labor is not in vain in the Lord."

—1 CORINTHIANS 15:58

Winston Churchill once gave a speech at the college he attended, that was to be the shortest, yet most remembered of all his speeches. The entire speech consisted of only six words, "Never, never, never, never, never quit!" (Churchill n.d.)

Stand firm in your commitment. You must develop "stick-to-it-ness".

Until you commit to a venture, task or goal, there is a tendency to hesitate. A completely made up mind is the anecdote to hesitation.

Napoleon Hill's book, *Think and Grow Rich*, tells the story of a little girl who made up her mind to be fully committed to what she wanted:

> Shortly after Mr. Darby received his degree from the "University of Hard Knocks," and had decided to profit by his experience in the gold mining business, he had the good fortune to be present on an occasion that proved to him that "no" does not necessarily mean no.
>
> One afternoon he was helping his uncle grind wheat in an old-fashioned mill. The uncle operated a large farm on which a number of black sharecrop farmers lived. Quietly, the door was opened, and a small black child, the daughter of a tenant, walked in and took her place near the door.
>
> The uncle looked up, saw the child, and barked at her roughly, "What do you want?"
>
> Meekly, the child replied, "My mammy say send her fifty cents."
>
> "I'll not do it," the uncle retorted, "now you run on home."
>
> "Yes sir," the child replied. But she did not move.
>
> The uncle went ahead with his work, so busily engaged that he did not pay enough attention to the child to observe that

she did not leave. When he looked up and saw her still standing there, he yelled at her, "I told you to go on home! Now go, or I'll take a switch to you."

The little girl said, "Yes sir," but she did not budge.

The uncle dropped a sack of grain he was about to pour into the mill hopper, picked up a barrel stave, and started toward the child with an expression on his face that indicated trouble.

Darby held his breath. He was certain he was about to witness an assault. He knew his uncle had a fierce temper.

When the uncle reached the spot where the child was standing, she quickly stepped forward one step, looked up into his eyes, and screamed at the top of her shrill voice, "My mammy's gotta have that fifty cents!"

The uncle stopped, looked at her for a minute, then slowly laid the barrel stave on the floor, put his hand in his pocket, took out half a dollar, and gave it to her.

The child took the money and slowly backed toward the door, never taking her eyes off the man whom she had just conquered. After she had gone, the uncle sat down on a box and looked out the window into space for more than ten minutes. He was pondering, with awe, over the whipping he had just taken. (Hill 1960)

This child had a "made up" mind and was completely committed to getting the fifty cents for her mother. The "no" answer was not an option.

As I write this topic on commitment, I have this challenge of taking on a vision that is bigger than I. Sometimes I feel that I am completely alone in this venture. It is not easy to stand alone when the crowd is going in the opposite direction.

There will be a time when you will come to a crossroad of your commitment and a decision will have to be made. At this point, a decision has to be made to continue with your vision. Our prayers to God for help will give us power. Life has a strange way of testing our resolve. Our relationship with God is crucial because without God, we at times get weak. But God has a way of encouraging us when we are low in spirit. Remember, God wants us to be committed to our vision. He wants the glory during and after we have reached our destination. A high degree of commitment is the reason ordinary men do great things. All great men struggle at one time or another before they reach their destination.

I believe one has to be totally committed to God to do something great in life. Moses was totally committed to the vision God gave him to free the Israelite children from bondage, just as Noah was completely committed to God in building the ark. Daniel had to be committed to God in order to lie in the lions' den. The three Hebrews, Shadrach, Meshach and Abednego, showed their commitment to God as they were led in a fiery furnace. Because of Abraham's commitment to God, he agreed to sacrifice Isaac, his son on the altar.

Commitment is a "made up" mindset that a predetermined goal or outcome will be attained.

"A man is not doing much until the cause he works for possesses all there is of him."
—JOHN WANAMAKER

"No life will ever be great until it is dedicated and disciplined."
—PETER C. B. BYNOL

Commitment usually begins in an atmosphere of struggle. Very seldom do we see strong commitment arise out of a context of prosperity. Squandered time, wasted living, and distorted values may come out of prosperity, but commitment does not.

- When we make a commitment to study God's Word, God makes a commitment to us.

- We will only become great when we are committed to something.

- Greatness is a result of commitment.

- When we make a silent commitment to a definite purpose, we are destined to succeed.

Focusing your life

Focusing your energies in a single direction can work wonders. If you want something badly enough, long enough, and consistently enough, don't be surprised when you get it.

It is said that most people can stay focused on a dream for a year. A few people can stay focused for several years. But a winner will stay focused on a dream regardless as to how long it takes, to make that dream a reality.

In order to reach any worthwhile goal, it will require us to stay focused until the task is complete. As we focus, all of our energies are honed in on one object, somewhat like a laser beam.

When we give our full attention to an object, we are focused. The more definite and focused we are, the easier it is for us to make better decisions on our priorities and the use of our time.

Remember, without God, we can do nothing. With God, we can do all things. We can accomplish many things—great and mighty—when we focus on God.

"You will accomplish many things—great and mighty—when you keep your focus on God."
—CHARLES STANLEY

Perfect peace comes when you fix your mind on God. You must discipline yourself to meditate on God's presence and His Word. You will have a greater sense of God's presence and provision as you fix your mind on Him.

No one wants his problems to grow. However, the more time spent focusing on the problem, the bigger the problem seems to grow.

Instead, keep your focus on God. Delight yourself in Him, and seek His council. He will show you the solution. Remember, He promised that He would give you the desires of your heart.

THOUGHTS TO MEDITATE UPON
TO PREPARE FOR GOD'S ABUNDANT LIFE:

- Focus only on the things you want, never on the things you don't want.
- You give power to what you focus on.
- Focus on God to succeed.
- What you focus on, you give your undivided attention and interest.

How to stay happy and young forever

IT IS WRITTEN:

"Jesus said, 'I have come that they may have life, and that they may have it more abundantly."

—JOHN 10:10

The happiest people in the world are those people who are living out their life-long dreams. They have engrossed their lives in something bigger than they are.

It's the "dream" that keeps us young; it's the "vision" that keeps us going. I believe that when we are engaged on a vision course, the mind is constantly sending messages throughout the body to sustain the necessary health for the vision at hand.

Dreams and visions send messages throughout the entire body. When there are no visions or dreams, there are no messages to the body to promote and sustain the necessity for renewing one's body, mind, soul, or spirit—important factors for promoting the will to live.

I believe that when a person has a dream and a vision in the forefront at all times, that person will always remain youthful and happy. Why? The mind is the controlling mechanism for the entire body. The mind dictates what messages will be received by the body. Consequently, the body will always obey all messages sent to it by the brain, whether they are positive or negative. The body acts like a servant to the mind, and the mind is like the master to the entire body which also includes the mind.

A vision or dream gives our life a purpose to exist—a cause to live. It inspires us to continue with vigor, enthusiasm and excitement for the rest of our life. And above all, a dream exudes power to the mind and body to help manifest the dream.

It is written:

"Blessed are the pure in heart. For they shall see God."
—Matthew 5:8

Complete and total happiness, however, can only be found through the Holy Spirit. If you desire a totally fulfilled and complete sense of happiness in your life, you must always strive to live a holy life.

It is written:

"But just as He who called you is holy, so be holy in all you do; for it is written: 'Be holy, because I am holy.'"
—1 Peter 1:15-16(NIV)

Thoughts to meditate upon
to Prepare for God's Abundant Life:

- Always think young and let this thought become a habit.
- When you think young, the brain sends this message throughout the body.
- Get involved in some activity to keep the mind occupied and engaged (i.e., dancing, exercise, swimming, aerobics, or roller skating).

Giving to the work of God

To tithe is to give ten percent of your income towards God's work. When you believe that God owns everything, giving back a portion of your earnings (as well as your time) to further the work of God demonstrates your gratitude and appreciation for all He has blessed you with. You should consider tithing as an investment into God's kingdom, with an expectation of a return on the investment.

The Bible tells us that everything is based on seedtime and harvest. Just as the farmer plants seeds in the ground and waits patiently for the harvest, so should you plant seeds for God's work as you wait patiently to reap the benefits and rewards of God's kingdom.

IT IS WRITTEN:

"While the earth remains, seedtime and harvest, cold and heat, winter and summer, and day and night shall not cease."

—Genesis 8:22

The church is set up to do the work of God. Your tithes are used in God's kingdom to do God's work. When you receive the Word of God from your pastor, you should make a commitment to the continued teachings of God's Word through tithing to your church. As you reap the benefits of God's kingdom here on earth through the receiving of counseling, fellowship, teaching, or spiritual nourishment through your church, you should give thanks by giving back to your church through tithing. When you do not tithe, you cannot be certain of the harvest.

As a believer, you should set a goal to give at least ten percent of your income for the benefit of the church. The church has financial requirements that must be met on a monthly basis in order to continue doing the work of God, and be available to meet the needs of God's people. Without giving and tithing, the church cannot survive.

Whether you give of your time, treasures, or talents, the Bible reminds us to give cheerfully.

IT IS WRITTEN:

"So let each one give as he purposes in his heart, not
grudgingly or of necessity; for God loves a cheerful giver."
— 2 CORINTHIANS 9:7

Bear in mind, tithing alone will not always, yield a harvest if you are disobedient in other areas of your life. If you have a flaw in your character, God may see fit to block your expected harvest. For example, if a believer is abusing his mate verbally or physically, God may block his harvest to get the believer's attention. Why should God bless the believer when he is in disobedience to God's Word. Why should God bless you fully and abundantly if you give sparingly and live in defiance of God's laws and will? God's desire is for you to seek excellence in character.

IT IS WRITTEN:

"But this I say, he who sows sparingly will also reap
sparingly, and he who sows bountifully will also reap
bountifully."
—2 CORINTHIANS 9:6

"And God is able to make all grace abound toward
you, that you, always having all sufficiency in all things,
may have an abundance for every good work."
—2 CORINTHIANS 9:8

THOUGHTS TO MEDITATE ON
TO PREPARE YOU FOR GODS ABUNDANT LIFE

- The believer should aim at giving at least ten percent of his income to the church.
- Plant your offering as a seed into the kingdom of God.
- Use your seed as an investment into the work of God with an expectation of a return on the investment.
- Give to God and expect an abundant life. However, the abundant life comes with conditions (i.e. excellence of character and obedience to the commandments of God).
- To love God, yourself, and others is the summation of the first and second commandments of God.

8

ooooo

SETTING GOALS FOR WEALTH

"One thing I always do, forgetting the past and straining toward what is ahead, I keep trying to reach the goal and get the prize for which God called me through Christ to the life above."

— PHILIPPIANS 3:13-14

When you have goals, you do not have to drift aimlessly through the days, weeks, months, and years of your life. In order to achieve your goals, you must understand what preparation it will take to accomplish them. You must plan each step or activity it will take to reach your goal, and the time frame it will take to accomplish them. Without a plan, chances are you will not accomplish anything.

If you are going to accomplish something, why not plan to accomplish something big. People are measured by the size of their dreams. But, you must remember to set goals to get things done.

Intense goals can keep a person alive and young. Regardless of the size of your goal, it will require taking one-step at a time to achieve it. You do not have to set out to accomplish only one big goal. Keep in mind that to accomplish a big goal, requires the achievement of a series of little goals.

The important thing is to set realistic goals for yourself, so that you will be able to feel a sense of accomplishment; and be empowered to set bigger long-term goals. Judge the things you do daily and ask this question: "Will this task help take me where I want to go?" If your answer is no, back off. No one can make one big jump to success. We get there one-step at a time.

A good plan is to start by setting short-term goals (i.e., monthly, weekly, daily) to accomplish. You must visualize your goal to realize your goal. If you cannot see the possibility or feasibility of reaching your goal, reduce the size of your goal to make continuous progress. Once you have been able to successfully accomplish your short-term goals, visualize, and write a plan to achieve long-term goals (i.e., ten year, five year, or one-year goals).

Remind yourself that you must have a clear fix on where you want to go. It is not important where you are now or where you have been. What matters is where you are going.

You should set goals relative to your visions, dreams, spiritual growth, family, vocation, social, and financial independence. Your goals should become a part of you. Practice meditating on each goal from time to time, in order to keep the goal embedded into your subconscious mind.

By meditating on your goals, you aid in the mental or spiritual development, and contemplation of your goal. As you gain greater spiritual insight and guidance, and become more relaxed in the pursuit of your goals, your subconscious will, in time, receive and act on your goal. Everything you need to make your goal a reality will be attracted to you.

You now have the most effective way to achieve any goal. You will be able to do those things that pertain to your goals. Your subconscious mind is the seat of all your habits. It is the things you do as habits that will make you successful in attaining your goals.

For example, once we learn how to drive a car, our subconscious mind aids us in becoming a good driver. We can be highly successful and winners in everything we do, only when we have fully engaged the subconscious mind. An average person with average talent, ambition, and education can outstrip the most brilliant genius in our society, if that person has clear, focused goals.

Goals in writing are dreams with deadlines.

"Committing your goals to pen and paper increases the likelihood of your achieving them by one thousand percent."
—Brian Tracy

"The great breakthrough in your life comes when you realize that you can learn anything you need to learn to accomplish any goal that you set for yourself. This means there are no limits on what you can be or do."
—Brian Tracy

Too often people engage in activities that are tension relieving rather than goal achieving. Set peace of mind as your highest goal and organize your entire life around it.

Believe that when you set a goal to live your life according to the Word of God, you have greater assurance of receiving the happiness and success in life that you desire, and that God desires for you. Always visualize your goals with God beside you and within you. Reach for the sky—you will achieve them.

"It's pretty hard for the Lord to guide you if you haven't made up your mind which way you want to go."
—Madame C. J. Walker

"Your goal should be out of reach but not out of sight."
—Anita Defrantz

Thoughts to meditate upon
to Prepare for God's Abundant Life:

- Examine yourself. Think of what can you do to become more effective.

- Concentrate on one or more short-term goals that you can accomplish. Identify the strategies and tactics you must undertake to accomplish each, and write them down. Were you successful?

- Concentrate on one or more long-term goals that you can accomplish. Identify the strategies and tactics you must undertake to accomplish each, and write them down with a projected timeline. Were you successful?

- Do you know your purpose in life? How do they align with your goals?

Imagination

Every believer has his own personal laboratory in his mind; it is his imagination. What you can imagine, you can accomplish. This laboratory marks the power of the imagination. This imagination is a gift of God. It is also one of the attributes of God. If God can imagine it, so can you. You were given the power to create, imagine, rule, have dominion on earth, speak things into existence, and overcome problems of the world.

The imagination of man has played a part in the creation of every fabricated object on earth. Every heavenly body that we see was at one time in the imagination of God, and God spoke into existence the heavens and earth.

IT IS WRITTEN:

"In the beginning God created the heaven and the earth."
—GENESIS 1:1

There is power in the imagination, because the thing imagined can be transformed into reality. If the mind of man can imagine a thing, the mind of man can achieve it.

"The source and center of all man's creative power is his power of making images, or the power of imagination."
—ROBERT COLLIER

"The mind must see visual achievement of the purpose before action is initiated."
—MARK R. DOUGLAS

"Visualize this thing that you want. See it, feel it, believe in it. Make your mental blueprint, and begin to build it."
—ROBERT COLLIER

THOUGHTS TO MEDITATE UPON
TO PREPARE FOR GOD'S ABUNDANT LIFE:

- Use your imagination to see yourself with your goals already accomplished.

- Use your imagination to see yourself winning in everything you do.

- Use your imagination to see yourself succeeding.

Let God direct your path and your plans for life

The dictionary defines a plan as a "system for achieving objective—a method of doing something that is worked out in advance." (Microsoft Corporation 2009)

IT IS WRITTEN:

"In all your ways acknowledge Him and He shall direct your paths."

—PROVERBS 3:6

"A man's heart plans his way, but the Lord directs his steps."

—PROVERBS 16:9

As a believer, you should always let others view your plans to increase the probability of success. It is wise to bring several minds in on an endeavor.

Knowing what you want is not enough, but it is the first step to success. The second step is to lay out a plan for its attainment. The third step is to set goals to measure the progress.

Next, ask God to help you plan, set goals and attain the object you are pursuing. Ask God to guide you not only in your professional life, but in your personal and family life as well.

IT IS WRITTEN:

"Plans are established by counsel."
—PROVERBS 20:18

"A good plan is like a road map; it shows the final destination and usually marks the best way to get there."
—H. STANLY JUDD

"Your life can't go according to plans if you have not planned."
—NIARA SUDASKASA

"With a definite, step by step plan —oh, what a difference it makes; you cannot fail because each step carries you along to the next like a track."
—SCOTT REED

"Every well built house started in the form of a definite purpose plus a definite plan in the nature of a set of blueprints."
—NAPOLEON HILL

At the beginning of your planning process, it is important to understand what God wants for you. He has given each of you gifts and talents that suggest His purpose for you on earth.

Once you know what it is that God wants you to do, set goals. Specify immediate goals, mid-range goals and long-range goals.

Begin your goal setting session in prayer and listen to God as He directs you in the way to proceed. God will bring the right desires to your heart. The desires that God brings to your heart is what He wants you to do with your life.

You must always depend on God to direct you on your path, to be all that He purposed you to be. God will always be there to keep you on track.

You and I, have a life to live. God gave us both a purpose. This purpose is a mission that must be fulfilled. You and I will not have life's intended joy and peace until our work is purpose driven.

Most people know where they are in life, yet, they are lost. They need direction. This happens because they are not following a plan. When a person has a plan, he knows where he is going.

When you know where you are going and you are occupied on your journey, it seems as if all of life's forces, whatever they are, will come to your aid. This is the work of your sovereign God. He is there to help you at all times, because His master plan for each of us is to contribute towards making this world a better place to live, and building the kingdom of God.

Thoughts to meditate upon
to Prepare for God's Abundant Life:

- Make your plans for where you want to be in the next year.
- Ask God to guide your steps in planning and execution.
- If you decide to work without a plan, you are winging it and this leads to failure.

9

ooooo

Paying the Price for Wealth

"Yet it shall not be so among you: but who ever desires to become great among you, let him be your servant."

—Matthew 20:26

There is a price to pay for all great achievements. Every person who has attained greatness had to pay the price of constant struggles, setbacks, battles, and disappointments. I am reminded of all the successes that God allowed me to accomplish in my life that came only after a price of diligent work, prayers, and faith.

During my real estate investing days, I had to search for the right property to invest in. After the property was renovated, I had to locate a buyer. This process was repeated several times before a substantial profit was realized.

Every study of high achieving men and women proves that greatness in life is only possible when you become outstanding in your chosen field. Only those who resolve to pay the price and make the necessary sacrifice will get into the top ten percent in their field. This is the approach of all great individuals and the payoff is incredible.

Never be reluctant to give of yourself generously when you are pursuing any endeavor. It is the mark of caring, compassion, and personal greatness. The Bible tells you to pursue a task as if you are doing it for the Lord.

Success will come when you do what you love to do, and commit to being the best in your field. I have discovered that there are no secrets to success or greatness, only timeless principles that have proven effective throughout the centuries.

Success in your career or business will come when you make yourself valuable and indispensable. Greatness will come in your life when you deliberately pursue it. Make a decision today to be great.

Most people will settle for living a mediocre life. I do believe that one gets what one pays for. If you pay a small price in life to achieve success, you will get a small reward. If on the other hand a substantial price is paid for success, a higher degree of success is likely.

"This I do know beyond any reasonable doubt. Regardless of what you are doing, if you will pump long enough, hard enough and enthusiastically enough, sooner or later the effort will bring forth the reward."

— Zig Zigler

In my life, there has been a constant struggle and a ceaseless battle to bring about success—many times from inhospitable surroundings. However, as believers, we must be reminded that there will always be a price to pay for all great achievements. At times you may need to spend more time away from your family than you like, work on weekends, miss a child's track meet or baseball game, or work late nights to meet a project due date. You may find yourself having to go the extra mile and assume more responsibility than others to get a task completed.

Thoughts to meditate upon to Prepare for God's Abundant Life:

- Nothing of value will come to the believer without a price.
- Make up your mind to succeed and persist until you do, no matter what the cost dictates.
- Every great achievement is the accumulation of many ordinary efforts.
- Every believer has the opportunity to become great because he has some of the attributes of God in him.

Living with courage

Courage is the power to face difficulties! The Lord instructed Joshua to be strong and have good courage.

IT IS WRITTEN:

"Be strong and of good courage, do not fear nor be afraid of them, for the Lord your God, He is the One who goes with you, He will not leave you or forsake you."
—DEUTERONOMY 31:6

God desires His children to show courage and strength in the face of difficulties. Strength and courage of the believer comes from God alone.

All of you will face difficulties in life. God knows what you need in times of trials and He will always provide you courage to meet the trial.

We as God's children can trigger the courage we need by standing on the promises of God. We draw strength from God's promises.

Courage is the opposite of being discouraged. Courage comes from a reservoir in the mind that is much more powerful than any circumstance.

IT IS WRITTEN:

"Be of good courage and He shall strengthen your heart. All you who hope in the Lord."
—PSALM 31:24

When we face difficulties, we can go to God for help and the God within us reminds us that we are bigger than our problems. He inspires us to gain the courage necessary to win.

Courage is having the right attitude about God's promises. In time of need, we draw upon the promises of God. We know that we can rely on God's Word.

David recalled how God had strengthened him in the past to kill a lion and a bear. He expected the same help from God to kill Goliath. David knew that God is always faithful and therefore he could rely on Him.

We, as God's children can always rely on God. He is faithful and unchanging. I believe that God will train His children to trust Him. He will sometimes place you in situations, or put new opportunities before you that require you to have faith, believe and trust in God—knowing that He can and will see you through.

He does this to teach and remind you to call on and depend on Him. You must believe in your reliance on God, as our faithful and unchanging Father.

We were made in the "Image of God" with His many attributes. Because we are winners in Christ, we can be courageous in all things.

IT IS WRITTEN:

"I am the vine, you are the branches. He who abides in Me, and I in him, bears much fruit; for without Me you can do nothing."
—JOHN 15:5

God has also given believers the power to rule over many things on the earth, including our own thoughts, fears, weaknesses, and more. Courage and power each reflect a status of man's mental or physical capacities to overcome feelings of anxiety, inadequacy, and self-doubt to rise above any situation. Obstacles should always look larger to a non-believer than to a believer, because the Holy Spirit lives in the believer who has the power to overcome.

You must maintain the attitude, that with God you can do all things. This is how God wants His children to think. Continued study, and strengthening of your faith and belief in God will enable you to develop greater courage and power to overcome and achieve.

IT IS WRITTEN:

"I can do all things through Christ who strengthens me."

—PHILIPPIANS 4:13

Remember, God has given you all that you need to master anything on the earth that is within God's will. The more you trust in the Lord's presence within you, the more secure you will feel, and the more courageous you will become even in the most trying of circumstances.

Man is not the creature of circumstances. Circumstances are the creature of man. You have the God given power to dominate over any circumstance. When in doubt, pray on it. God is available anytime to hear your prayers.

THOUGHTS TO MEDITATE UPON
TO PREPARE FOR GOD'S ABUNDANT LIFE:

- Courageous believers look to God and trust Him.

- Courageous believers recall past experiences of victories.

- Courageous believers never look for ways to escape. They know that God will never leave them.

- Courageous believers always have victory.

- Think "courage" in everything you do.

- God instructs His children to have courage.

- Let courage be a habit in your life.

- Power comes in the believer's life when there is courage.

- When the believer focuses on God, He has power and courage.

- A lack of courage means a lack of knowledge in knowing who you are in Christ.

- God's Word is alive. When we take the Word in us, there is a renewing of the mind. There should be a renewed courage mindset in the believer.

- When in doubt, pray on it. God will answer your prayers.

Developing good habits

Throughout our lives, most of us will develop some form of behavior that demonstrates a tendency toward an action or condition, which by repetition has become involuntary—a habit. Habits can work for us or against us. Good habits can make you successful and bad habits can lead to poverty.

Believers can walk as children of light in all goodness, righteousness, and truth. This habit will always exalt Him.

You can intentionally practice certain activities or behaviors to establish a desired habit. Be careful not to repeat certain actions or behaviors that become bad habits.

"The individual who wants to reach the top in business must appreciate the might of the force of habit and must understand that practices are what create habits. He must be quick to break those habits that can break him — and hasten to adopt those practices that will help him achieve the success he desires."

—J. Paul Getty

Highly successful people tend to have many more good habits than bad ones. A habit is an involuntary practice.

"We first make our habits; and then our habits make us."
—Horace Mann

"Sow an act — reap a habit;
Sow a habit — reap a character;
Sow a character — reap a destiny."
—George Dana Boardman

"Habit, my friend, is practice long pursued, that at last becomes the man himself."

—Evenus

- Success comes as a series of good habits.
- Habits are involuntary actions.
- Make it a habit to love everyone.
- Make it a habit to sow good seeds daily.

Procrastination in your life

One of the greatest obstacles in the believer's life is probably putting things off that need to be done. It is much easier to do nothing, than it is to act. The Devil, an enemy of the believer, will give you all the reasons to put something off to a later time.

Procrastination can be a direct hindrance to your progress, especially if it has become a habit in your daily life. Action is the best antidote to putting things off to a later time. You can train yourself to ensure progress in life by taking action. The more you do today, the less you will have to do tomorrow. Conversely, the less you do today, the more you will have to do tomorrow. Goals and deadlines are not met mainly because of procrastination.

Having a passionate spirit about your future is a great way to conquer procrastination. Having a burning desire to attain a goal is another way to keep procrastination under control.

Develop a daily checklist for staying in control of getting important things done. This will help to defeat procrastination in your life.

Thoughts to meditate upon to Prepare for God's Abundant Life:

- Become an action person.
- Do not put off until tomorrow anything you can do today.
- Recognize that procrastination is a negative progress.

10

PREPARING FOR WEALTH

*"Prepare your outside work, make it fit for
yourself in the field; and afterward build your house."*

—PROVERBS 24:27

Fortune and fame favor the prepared individual. Fortune, on the other hand, does not wait for the person who is not prepared.

Being prepared is "doing your homework." Academic study, on the job training, researching your field, learning your marketplace, and doing the groundwork that support your endeavors, visions, passions, dreams, etc. represent the preparation needed in any pursuit

There is no greater power, than in that of a person who is prepared. Luck, if you believe in it, favors the one who is ready to act.

"Some say opportunity knocks only once. That is not true. Opportunity knocks all the time, but you have to be ready for it. If the chance comes, you must have the equipment to take advantage of it."
—Louis L'Amour

"Take a second look at what appears to be someone's "good luck." You find not luck but preparation, planning, and success — producing thinking."
—David Joseph Schwartz

"When you prepare for a thing, the opportunity to use it presents itself."
—Edgar Cayce

"The secret of success in life is for a man to be ready for his opportunity when it comes."
—Benjamin Disraeli

"The way to success is through preparation. It don't just happen. You don't wake up one day and discover you're a lawyer anymore than you wake up as a pro football player. It takes time."
—Alan Page

And remember: "Success is difficult; it's gut—wrenching and pain—inducing."
—Parren Mitchell

In the final analysis, you are responsible for being prepared to become successful in life.

- An ounce of prevention is better than a pound of cure.
- When you prepare, you save time, effort and in many cases money.
- When we ask God for something that is in His will, we demonstrate faith by preparing for it.

The bible is a success manual

After reading many books over the years on self-improvement, it occurred to me that most of these success books got their origin from the Bible.

The Bible, in one sense, is a Master Success Manual. The Bible is a "self-help book" for the educated, the leader, the businessperson, the scientist, the achiever, the married, and anyone simply in need of spiritual guidance and support. Most importantly, the Bible is a "self-help book" for the brokenhearted, the incarcerated, the hospitalized, the addict, the divorced, the oppressed, the disenfranchised, and anyone simply in need of healing.

Once you have studied the Bible and all of God's promises for the believer, you have the knowledge to become wealthy. However, you must continue to abide in God's Word, and allow God's Word to abide in you.

Jesus proclaimed in the Bible that the poor people needed the gospel to be preached to them. The poor need to hear the knowledge of wealth. They did not have this knowledge; therefore, without knowledge the poor would remain poor.

IT IS WRITTEN:

"My people perish for the lack of knowledge."
—HOSEA 4:6

As believers, you should embrace the Bible as a manual to know God and to develop a relationship with Jesus. Through your relationship, you will be able to accomplish big things in life if you put God's business before your own. As you draw closer to God, by abiding in His Word, more will be revealed to you.

All that you desire is wrapped up in the embodiment of Jesus Christ. All good things on earth flow from God for the enjoyment of His children. You may enjoy them, but you must always remember to give thanks and glory to God for them.

THOUGHTS TO MEDITATE UPON
TO PREPARE FOR GOD'S ABUNDANT LIFE:

- Always rely on God's promises.
- Study the Bible to know all about God's Word and His promises.
- Read the Bible for knowledge.
- Study the Bible for self-improvement.

You are a winner in Christ

You can walk in victory everyday when Jesus is your example, and His Spirit lives within you. When you were saved and adopted into the family of God, you became a winner. Your new mindset should be:

IT IS WRITTEN:

"I can do all things through Christ, who strengthens me."

—PHILIPPIANS 4:13

In everything you do, God wants the glory. He is with you at all times. You are never alone.

IT IS WRITTEN:

"I will never leave you nor forsake you."

— HEBREWS 13:5

You should always have the mindset that you are a winner in all things, because God says you are. You should lead your life with a personal mantra, such as "I am a winner, I am a dream fulfiller, I am a conqueror, I am courageous, I am confident, and more—because God is within me."

Winning is not about abiding in your own strength. Remember your skills and power come from the Lord. Once you have adopted your "God presence," there is nothing to stand in your way.

God wants us to be victorious in all we undertake. The next time you face a challenge, acknowledge Him, and say aloud, "I can do all things through Christ who strengthens me."

"In all your ways acknowledge Him, and He shall direct your path."

—Proverbs 3:6

God is infinite and we are finite. When we fully rely on Him, we are tapping into His infinite power.

Obedience to God's Word is one of the conditions that must be met to receive any of God's promises. In addition to your being obedient to God's Word, He is also interested in your character.

"If a man has built a sound character, it makes but little difference what people say about him, he will win at the end."
— Napoleon Hill

In everything you do, think to yourself "I'll win." As a child of God, you can be assured to have the confidence and courage to win.

Thoughts to meditate upon
to Prepare for God's Abundant Life:

- Winners believe in the presence of God within.
- Winners keep the "big picture" in mind.
- Winners welcome a challenge with optimism.
- Winners do not waste time with unproductive thoughts.
- Winners focus on the task at hand

11

_{○○○○○}

Your Self-image and Wealth

"For we are His workmanship, created in Christ Jesus for good works, which God prepared beforehand that we should walk in them."

— Ephesians 2:10

You were at one time, a thought in the mind of God. He made you for His purpose and He has a plan for you on earth.

IT IS WRITTEN:

"For I know the plans I have for you, declares the Lord, plans to prosper you and not to harm you, plans to give you hope and a future."
—JEREMIAH 29:11(NIV)

Every human being was made by God for a particular purpose and plan. Everything that is done by God is in "divine order." God made every creature on this earth for a purpose. Every planet has a purpose. Only God himself knows the purpose of everything He made.

Man is the only creature that God made that can seek Him. God created you to do great and mighty things. Your self-image will always improve once you know and believe what God says about you as His offspring.

IT IS WRITTEN:

"I will praise You, for I am fearfully and wonderfully made; marvelous are Your works and that my soul knows very well."
—PSALM 139:14

You should have the same feelings about yourself that God feels about you. It is a sad thing that you may believe what others think about you over that which God says about you in His Word. God says that you can do all things with the aid of His Son Jesus Christ.

IT IS WRITTEN:

"I can do all things through Christ who strengthens me."
— PHILIPPIANS 4:13

We often tend to think in limitation about what we can do. God says in His Word, "through His son, there are no limitations."

As a believer, you should think about yourself, as God thinks about you. God made you, and only He knows what you can do. Your self-image should be positive and courageous.

In everything that you do, affirm daily, "I can do all things through Christ who strengthens me." This affirmation should be embedded in your subconscious until it becomes a part of your daily habit. It has been said it takes about twenty-one days for a new idea to become a habit. So repeat this affirmation aloud for twenty-one days.

Thoughts to meditate upon to Prepare for God's Abundant Life:

- We should see ourselves as God sees us.
- When we have a "God mind-set," we will always think right about ourselves.
- Allowing God's Word to abide in us always, gives us a healthy outlook on life.
- Focusing on God will give us a healthy "self image."

What do you think about you?

- We often cheat ourselves of the lives we could live, because we are too afraid of trying. If we knew ourselves better, we would fear less and accomplish more.

- It is important that each of you hold a mental picture of the person you want to become. As you maintain this image in your mind, thoughts are produced about the image you hold of yourself. Eventually, these thoughts become a part of your subconscious mind. The subconscious is the part of the brain where all habits are formed. Your thoughts can manifest themselves in your life and will attract all the energy and power from the universe to become the person you image.

IT IS WRITTEN:

"As a man thinketh in his heart so is he."
-- PROVERBS 23:7

You should view yourself as God sees you. God sees you as being righteous because of the shed blood of His son Jesus Christ. You have been fully forgiven of all sins. God said it and you should believe that "through Christ, you can do all things." You should be number one in all competitions. Why? Because God has empowered you with the Holy Spirit and given you all of that He has promised.

God sees you as a conqueror and achiever because of what Jesus has done. As a believer, you have the power of God living inside of you.

You can call on God at anytime. God will always be there. It is great to know that God is there to help you at anytime.

You should learn to believe that you could become best in everything you endeavor. You should never feel inferior. At the same time, you should never display pride—only humbleness and thankfulness. God is the true source of all you will ever need. God made you to be a winner and to overcome all obstacles through Christ.

No one can ever reach his maximum potential, and no one ever will without the Holy Spirit. However, as a child of God, you have a better chance in becoming all that you can be, when you use the power of God that lives inside you.

THOUGHTS TO MEDITATE UPON
TO PREPARE FOR GOD'S ABUNDANT LIFE:

- We should think about us the way God thinks about us.
- Guide your thoughts, because they lead to your destiny.
- The thoughts you have now are the seeds to your future.
- We are molded daily by the fabric of our thoughts.

To be born again

IT IS WRITTEN:

"Jesus answered and said to Nicodemus, a ruler of the Jews, 'Most assuredly, I say to you, unless one is born again, he cannot see the kingdom of God."
—JOHN 3:5

Jesus was speaking about being born of water and the Spirit, not of flesh. Once you have received Jesus as your personal Savior, the Holy Spirit comes immediately to dwell in your heart. When the Spirit of God becomes the center of your life, the Bible says you have been "born again."

When the Holy Spirit begins to work in your life, it enables you to hear God's voice. God will guide your decisions, move you through circumstances, and help you to fulfill plans to become the person God created you to be.

A person cannot become the person God created him or her to be as long as one is a nonbeliever. You must be born again.

God does not answer the prayers of nonbelievers, nor can they see the kingdom of God. All unsaved people are condemned by their own sin. Nonbelievers do not have everlasting life. There is no condemnation on the life of the believer. The shed blood of Jesus was the atonement for the believer's sin. God said that the sins of the believer have been forgotten, as if they never occurred. In essence, this means that all believers live in a state of righteousness.

It was God's will for Jesus to come to this earth to die for the sins of the world. God did this for one reason—love.

It is written:

"For God so loved the world that He gave His only begotten Son, that whoever believes in Him should not perish but have everlasting life."

— John 3:16

Thoughts to meditate upon
to Prepare for God's Abundant Life:

- Now that we know that we are loved unconditionally by God, we can ask God to help us as we set goals to be all that we can be.
- God placed you and I on this earth for His purpose. We can discover this purpose by seeking God in prayer.
- All of our daily thoughts should be centered around God.

God made you to last forever

God made man to live on earth and in heaven. Death, however, is not the end of you. It is not your termination. It is your transition into eternity. There is far more to life than the here and now. Even God's plans and purposes are forever. If you learn to love and trust God's Son Jesus, you will be invited to spend the rest of eternity with Him.

It is written:

"God has planted eternity in the heart of man."
— Ecclesiastes 3:11

"For we know that if our earthly house, this tent, is destroyed, we have a building from God, a house not made with hands, eternal in the heavens."
—2 Corinthians 5:1

"Surely God would not have created such a being as man to exist only for a day! No, no, man was made for immortality."
— Abraham Lincoln

Remember, everything that you do on earth will have eternal consequences. Your life here on earth is a testing ground for eternity. Think of it as a dress rehearsal for the final stage, which is in Heaven. All of God's children should be in preparation for the next life in heaven. Scripture reminds you, "This world is fading away, with everything it craves. But if you do the will of God, you will live forever."(1 John 2:17)

Thoughts to meditate upon
to Prepare for God's Abundant Life:

- God made our spirit to last forever.
- We will live with God forever.

12

RIGHTEOUS THOUGHTS FOR WEALTH

"As a man thinks in his heart, so is He."

— PROVERBS 23:7

All things in our universe can be traced to a single thought. Your thoughts are the result of your thinking process.

"Thoughts have power; thoughts are energy, and you can make your world or break it by your own thinking."
—Susan Taylor

Your thoughts about others that you encounter, will have some affect on how they react to you. When you hold and exhibit thoughts of kindness toward someone, they will most likely respond in kind manner. Conversely, when you display negative or resentful thoughts toward someone, their response will be similar.

It is said that your most dominating thoughts will determine your direction in life and that which you accomplish. I believe that you can become what you think as your thoughts will be manifested in your life in one way or another.

All wealth begins with thoughts. The amount of wealth you attain is only limited by your thoughts. Any limitation or obstacle you encounter, can be overcome by faithful thinking.

You must choose the right thoughts to achieve that which God wants for you. This will happen with a "God consciousness." This can happen through prayer. When you keep your mind stayed on God at all times, you are abiding in God's Word.

It is written:

"Pray without ceasing."
— 1 Thessalonians 5:17

When you are of a "God conscious," God will help to guide your your life. You will only become all that God intends for you when you accept His will—not your will.

God placed wealth on this earth for His children. He wants the best for His children, just as an earthly father desires the best for his children.

To receive God's abundance and wealth on the earth, you must earn it. Having a business, a career, or investments are just a few of the many ways that wealth can be received with His blessings.

Remember, "it is God who gives you the power to get wealth." God will teach you how to gain wealth in His Word. I believe that the first step in getting wealth is through His wisdom.

It is written:

"If any man lacks wisdom, let him ask of God who gives wisdom liberally."

— James 1:5

God also wants His children to be happy. Happiness is not just having wealth. Happiness is having a relationship with Jesus. He is your life and your friend. He said, He will "always be with us, and He will never leave us." (Hebrews 13:5).

God gave you the capacity to control your thought life. He made you in His image. God has thoughts and God can speak His thoughts into existence. God made us like Himself. We have thoughts and we can also speak our thoughts into existence. God said that "we shall have what we say." (Matthew 17:20)

Make sure you are saying in your thoughts and words what you want in your life. God gave you the choice to think negatively or positively. You should always strive to choose positive thoughts and words, for negative words will clothe themselves and be manifested in your life.

All wealth begins with the right positive thought. It is impossible to get wealth by choosing a negative thought. It just will not happen.

There is nowhere in the Bible that God used negative thoughts to accomplish anything. You have been told throughout the Bible to imitate God. This means to use positive thoughts and words to accomplish the things you desire in life.

God made it possible for you to tell if a goal or dream is attainable in your life. If you can visualize the dreams you desire, they can become dreams that you achieve. On the other hand, if you cannot see yourself attaining your dreams, you will not achieve them.

Close your eyes and try to see yourself already with your dream. Your dream could be to own a business, or a certain career or job. If you are able to actually see yourself with the accomplished dream, you can indeed have it. It is yours to go after.

On the other hand, try and see yourself standing in the living room of your home. Can you imagine your body levitating toward the ceiling and roof into the sky? Because you will not be able to envision this, the idea will be canceled by your imagination as a dream that you cannot actualize.

Thoughts are powerful! Why? Thoughts can have an effect on the material world. Thoughts can even travel from one mind to another. How many times have you been thinking about someone and the phone rings? To your surprise, it was the person you were thinking about.

Remember, you are like God our Father in many aspects. You are His offspring. When God sees you, He sees Jesus. You must also see yourself as a child of God.

You should be excited about your dreams, goals and visions in life. Why? Because you can make them a reality with God's help. God places dreams and desires in your thought process to help guide you. He desires to accomplish many things through you, His dear child. You seek not to let Him down.

God made you to win in life. However, you must choose to be a winner. He did not make you to be a robot. He made you like Himself. You have "free will" to choose to pursue your dreams. God will never force you to work toward your dreams. He has given you the power to think like Him. God is a Winner! He wants you to think like a winner.

Some thoughts seem to be impossibilities until they are realized.

"Thoughts lead to purposes; purposes go forth in action; actions form habits; habits decide character; and character fixes our destiny."
—TYRONE EDWARDS

THOUGHTS TO MEDITATE UPON
TO PREPARE FOR GOD'S ABUNDANT LIFE:

- Thoughts are the master builders to your destiny.
- Make sure your thoughts line up with where you want to be in the future.
- Your thoughts contain all the chapters of your life. Choose only those thoughts that will give you the life you will not regret.
- You should not waste one thought on anything that you do not want in your life.

Facing life with confidence

"It is better to trust God than to put confidence in man. "
— Psalm 118:8

As a believer, you should face life everyday with a very high degree of confidence. Why? You have the power and love of God dwelling inside of you. Your mindset each day should be to operate by the power of God, rather than by your own power.

You should feel and believe that you can do great things in life because God is with you and cheering for you, like an earthly father cheers for his son during a baseball game. The earthly father loves and wants the best for his son, just as God loves you and wants the best for you and all His children.

As a believer, you should feel as if you can conquer the world because you operate with the power of God. The unbeliever does not have God living on the inside, therefore he does not have access to the divine powers of God.

There are many advantages the believer has that the unbeliever does not have. Even though God loves both the same, the unbeliever has no assurance that God will help Him. The unbeliever cannot claim any of the promises that God has for His children. The unbeliever is not in the family of God. He will not be in the family of God until He accepts Jesus into his life.

The believer has the promise of eternal life with Christ. The unbeliever does not. Eternal life is only for people who have accepted Jesus Christ as their Savior.

Some of the advantages the believer has that the nonbeliever does not have are the power to be healed, protection from the Devil, peace, boldness and confidence in Jesus Christ. God has placed a limit on what the Devil can do to a believer.

God does not hear the prayers of the unbeliever. Why? Because the unbeliever is not in the family of God and God is not obligated to the request or petition of an unsaved person. Now there may be some occasions when God, through His Divine mercy, will help the unsaved person. This is solely up to the will of God. God does not promise in the scriptures that He will honor the prayers of any unsaved person.

It is written:

For He says to Moses, "I will have mercy on whomever I will have mercy and I will have compassion on whomever I will have compassion."

— Roman 9:15

Remember, the sins of the unsaved person have not been forgiven. There is no atonement, since the Shed Blood of Jesus does not cover the unsaved. God's Word says that sin must be punished. Since the unsaved person does not have Jesus in his life, his life is totally unprotected.

The believer lives under the protection of the Holy Spirit. Nothing can happen to you that God does not allow. Whatever God does permit, He will turn around for your good.

God's "grace" is not imparted to the unbeliever. God wants the unbeliever to repent and accept Jesus Christ into his life.

THOUGHTS TO MEDITATE UPON
TO PREPARE FOR GOD'S ABUNDANT LIFE:

- Develop the confident look — package yourself so that other people are interested in you.
- Build confidence with preparation.
- Tap your mind for victory memories.
- A loss is a lesson.
- To win, always state: "I am equal to the best."
- Recognize the "root" of fear — mismanaged thinking.
- Do what you fear and fear will disappear.
- God's Word should give every believer confidence.
- When we stand on God's promises, we are acting in faith.
- When we act in faith, we act in confidence.
- A sense of boldness will come from the believer who has indulged himself with God's Word.

How to start each day

IT IS WRITTEN:

"Acknowledge God in all your ways and He will direct your paths."

—PROVERBS 3:6

"Don't face the day until you've faced God."

—MAYA ANGELOU

Put God first at the beginning of the day by asking Him to lead you. Every day that dawns is a reason to say, "Thank You Father." You might start each day with a prayer similar to this:

"Father, I need You this day in my life to guide and direct my paths; for You know all things. You know what is best for me. As You go ahead of me this day, help me to follow Your plans and purpose for my life. I desire to accomplish as much for You as I can today to honor You. Help me to stay on course so that I progress speedily toward my vision and goal in Jesus' name."

THOUGHTS TO MEDITATE UPON
TO PREPARE FOR GOD'S ABUNDANT LIFE:

- Each day, place God first by asking Him to lead you.
- Acknowledge Him before your first assignment because God tells us to do this.
- Tell God that you know with Him you can do all things, and without Him, you can do nothing.

Enthusiasm in your life

Practice becoming enthusiastic about your life—be zealous and intensely excited about your life! Just as a great salesman understands that enthusiasm is key to a successful presentation, and a great orator understands that an enthusiastic delivery moves audiences; so should you understand that your zest for life and work will energize and motivate you and others to take action.

Enthusiasm is also a state of mind that inspires and arouses one to put action into the task at hand. Enthusiasm is contagious. When you are excited about your life and your work, others will become excited.

Any vision without enthusiasm will be a vision without much hope. However, when enthusiasm is added to the vision, everyone involved will be electrified and motivated to achieve the vision.

When you find yourself interested in something, dig in and learn more about it. Research and do more research. Why? You are activating an enthusiastic attitude. You are planting a seed of enthusiasm that will give you the right attitude that is necessary to have the winning edge. This technique lights up everything about you; your smile, your handshake, your talk, even your walk. You will not only act very much alive, you will have power to do things in a big way and win people to your way of thinking.

Use the "research more" technique to develop enthusiasm toward other people. Find out more about what they do, their background, and you will find your interest and enthusiasm about them mounting. Continue to dig and you will eventually discover a fascinating person.

Enthusiasm is actually energy in motion which equals power. It makes all the difference in the world. It gives you a much needed edge—enthusiasm makes you feel and act like a winner. When you feel like a winner, you are one step closer to winning.

THOUGHTS TO MEDITATE UPON
TO PREPARE FOR GOD'S ABUNDANT LIFE:

- When enthusiasm is used in reaching your goal, you will create power and energy that will help you attain your goal.
- Ask God to help you reach your goals.
- Stand on one of God's promises to give you confidence.

13

WEALTH COMES WITH WISDOM

"Wisdom is the principal thing; therefore get wisdom. And in all your getting, get understanding."

— PROVERBS 4:7

The Bible tells us that wisdom was with God from the beginning. God implores you to seek Him for wisdom, and He will gladly give it to you. Wisdom precedes success.

God is excited to give you wisdom. But when you ask Him for wisdom, you must ask in faith. You must believe that He will give you wisdom.

IT IS WRITTEN:

"If any of you lack wisdom, let him ask of God, who gives to all liberally and without reproach, and it will be given to him."
— JAMES 1:5

You can only become all that God intended for you by seeking Him for wisdom. It is wisdom that gives you the ability to discern and make sound judgments about your choices in life.

IT IS WRITTEN:

"The fear of the Lord is the beginning of wisdom."
— PROVERBS 9:10(NIV)

THOUGHTS TO MEDITATE UPON
TO PREPARE FOR GOD'S ABUNDANT LIFE:

- Think wisdom in everything today.
- Ask God for His help.
- Focus on wisdom and wisdom will be expanded in your life.

God's plan for your life

We can find God's plan for our life when we spend time getting to know Him.

The more intimate you become with God, the more you will know Him. He will reveal himself to you once you earnestly pursue Him. God will plant dreams, thoughts, and desires in your heart and mind that represent His intended purpose for you in life.

After you have walked with God for some time, you will begin to distinguish between your own thoughts and God's thoughts for you.

Remember, God made you and He gives you thoughts, which contain His purpose for your life. You can identify these thoughts from God once you get to know Him. You will not be able to recognize "God thoughts" if you do not know God. God will communicate Himself to you through your thoughts. God's thoughts for us are always positive and they are within us to draw us closer to Him.

Thoughts to meditate upon
to Prepare for God's Abundant Life:

- Ask God to impress upon your thoughts His plans and assignment for your life.
- By all means, get to know God in an intimate way.
- Acknowledge God in everything you do.
- Learn to listen to God!

Your spiritual growth

Once you are saved, God wants you to grow in grace, to become just like His Son Jesus. This is God's goal for you.

IT IS WRITTEN:

"But grow in the grace and knowledge of our Lord and Savior Jesus Christ. To Him be glory both now and forever!"

— 2 PETER 3:18(NIV)

God expects you to read His Word for the ongoing renewal of your mind and spirit to occur.

IT IS WRITTEN:

"And do not be conformed to this world, but be transformed by the renewing of your mind, that you may prove what is that good and acceptable and perfect will of God."

— ROMANS 12:2

Once you are saved, God gives you a new spirit. You should begin to meditate on God's Word to help develop and renew your mind, and to remove any unwanted rebellious and disobedient thoughts.

The Holy Spirit is both your Comforter and Helper as you grow in grace with our Lord and Savior, Jesus Christ. It is God's goal for all believers to have the "mind of Christ."

As a believer, you should always be ready to repent for any shortcomings or failures. Never try to cover up or deny your sins.

Remember God's goal for you is to become more Christ like. The Holy Spirit that lives inside of you will help you to tap into the power of God.

THOUGHTS TO MEDITATE UPON
TO PREPARE FOR GOD'S ABUNDANT LIFE:

- The Holy Spirit is my helper in time of need.
- The Holy Spirit is my comforter.
- You can tell the Holy Spirit what you desire.
- As you become more like Jesus, use the power of God that is in you.

You are in the family of God

The day you were saved you were grafted into the family of God. Every promise of God is now available to you. God is there to answer your prayers and to communicate to you through the Holy Spirit.

Once you are saved, God begins His cleansing process of your life. God's desire now, is to mold and shape your life like his Son Jesus. As a born again Christian, God wants you to represent Him just like an ambassador on earth. You are now God's representative and you must carry yourself as such. As a believer, you have a new home in heaven.

Jesus is our intercessor. He is sitting at the right hand of God. As a child of God, the believer has all the privileges of a family member. Every person on earth has needs, but God only promises to address the needs of His children. God's ear is tuned to whatever concerns His children. For God expresses His love for the believer and His promises are there for them to claim.

A believer in the family of God has power because you are a child of God. You are molded in the image of God and have some of the attributes of God. As a believer, you should think of the many things that you can do because you belong to God. God's power is available to you at all times.

The Bible is clear on God's promise, "I can do all things through Christ who strengthens me." (Philippians 4:13) You should believe that you can do all things, as the promise did not say "some things." This promise should become embedded in your mind, heart, and spirit so that you can do great and mighty things for God.

THOUGHTS TO MEDITATE UPON
TO PREPARE FOR GOD'S ABUNDANT LIFE:

- Only a believer can approach the throne of God in prayer.
- Because of the shed blood of Jesus, the believer's sins are forgiven.
- The believer has rights to the promises of God.
- The believer has a new home in heaven.

14

BUILDING RELATIONSHIPS FOR WEALTH

"There are many members, but one body. And the eye cannot say to the hand, I have no need of you; or again the head to the feet, I have no need of you."

—1 CORINTHIANS 12:20-21

One of the reasons for living is to have great relationships, and to have people you love and respect, who also love and respect you. There is not a single person alive who can say they do not need someone else. We all have a need for some type of relationship with another.

Every human being has at least one thing in common; a desire for success. That is why you must admit that you need other people in your life. In your career, job or business, think about how much your success depends upon others.

Just as relationships are necessary for you to be effective in everyday activities, so is it necessary for you to have a strong relationship with God to be effective and successful throughout life and all you endeavor. You must spend time with God so that you can hear from Him and know Him as an infinitely loving God.

At some point in life, you may feel moments of emptiness or loneliness. It is during these times you will find that a deeper relationship with Jesus will fill the void.

Sometimes, God will use adversity to pull you into a deeper relationship with Him. Adversity often brings you face to face with the need to associate with different people. Perhaps you need to develop new relationships with new Christian believers.

Highly successful business people will tell you the importance of having the right relationship with the right people. There is always someone who has in their possession exactly what you may need. Also, the person who has what you need has a need of their own.

Having the right relationships, seems to be the answer in all of my business dealings. Developing relationships is a key component of marketing and business growth.

One good way to develop a business relationship is to stay mindful that God says you are to help one another. Networking is a good way to aid one another in a business sense, because everyone has the chance to benefit from the network system.

When talking with someone, keep an ear open for that business person's needs. In doing so, you may be able to make a suggestion, or offer a referral to someone else who might be of assistance.

You can leverage yourself and others through relationship marketing. We all have something of value to offer if we know exactly what someone else needs. Many people have become wealthy by discovering a need and filling that need in the market place. Show me someone who is highly successful, and I will show you someone who has developed the right relationships.

Remember, God desires a "divine" relationship with you to draw you closer to Him so that you will know Him better. He wants a relationship with you to make you more like Jesus.

Look for the good in every person and every situation. You will almost always find it. Your ability to get along well with others will determine your happiness and success as much as any other factor.

Learn to identify various differences in people. For example, some women may tend to be more complex and subtle, while some men may be more direct and simplistic in their mannerisms or approach to business. Each, however, has value—and deserves your respect and attention.

"A great man shows his greatness by the way he treats the little man."
—CARLISLE

The value you place on people determines whether you are a motivator or a manipulator of men. Motivation is moving together for a mutual advantage. With the motivator, everybody wins. With the manipulator, only the leader wins.

Thoughts to meditate upon
to Prepare for God's Abundant Life:

- If we are to succeed big, we must build relationships.
- Be a relationship builder; specialize in promoting relationships.
- Never belittle any relationship.
- Love everyone to ensure great relationships.

Enjoyment in your life

It is written:

"So I commended enjoyment, because a man has nothing better under the sun than to eat, drink and be merry; for this will remain with him in his labor all the days of his life which God gives him under the sun."
— Ecclesiastes 8:15

God has made man's soul, spirit and mind to desire enjoyment. For it is the wellspring of life itself. It is the epitome of wealth and fame. Money is the root of enjoyment. We all seek it in one form or another. No one purposely rejects enjoyment.

Enjoyment is a benefit derived from God. He wants you to feel pleasure and enjoyment in your life.

"You will show me the path of life; In Your presence is fullness of joy; At Your right hand are pleasures forevermore."

—PSALM 16:11

Pleasure and enjoyment follows work, and prosperity.

"Success in its highest and noblest form calls for peace of mind and enjoyment and happiness which comes only to the man who has found the work that He likes best."

— NAPOLEON HILL

I am a firm believer that you should only do the work you enjoy doing. In doing so, you will be able to do your best and excel.

"A man must get his happiness out of his work ...without work he enjoys, he can never know what happiness is."

—THOMAS CARLYLE

"No man can succeed in a line of endeavor which he does not like."

—NAPOLEON HILL

"If you don't love something, then don't do it."

—RAY BRADBURY

"If you don't get a kick out of the job you're doing you'd better hunt for another one."

—SAMUEL VAN CLAIN

It is impossible to succeed in an endeavor that you don't like. How can you excel or prosper? You must honor God by displaying excellence in your endeavor.

IT IS WRITTEN:

"Whatever your hand finds to do, do it with your might; for there is no work or device or knowledge or wisdom in the grave where you are going."
—ECCLESIASTES 9:10

"When you eat the labor of your hands, you shall be happy, and it shall be well with you."
—PSALM 128:2

Let no man tell you that the gift of life is not for enjoyment. If it were not so, God would not have given you the capacity to experience enjoyment. You should wake up every day to experience the enjoyment of life that God has provided you. Enjoyment is a choice and a frame of mind. God has provided the basics for your enjoyment. You must choose the right attitude to be happy and hope that others close to you are happy too.

THOUGHTS TO MEDITATE UPON
TO PREPARE FOR GOD'S ABUNDANT LIFE:

- God wants His children to enjoy life.
- God will take care of His children by providing for them.
- We should enjoy the work we love to do. We only excel in the work we love.

The power of prayer in your life

As a believer, you have the right to go to God in prayer and ask for anything you need or desire. If your desires are within the will of God, you will receive that which you ask when you do not doubt God.

IT IS WRITTEN:

"But let him ask in faith, with no doubting, for he who doubts is like a wave of sea driven and tossed by the wind."

— JAMES 1:6

"The effective, fervent prayer of a righteous man avails much."

—JAMES 5:16b

God will always honor the prayers of His children. God knows that you will always have needs.

IT IS WRITTEN:

"In this world, you will always have trouble."

—JOHN 16:33

Prayer is how the power of God is unleashed. You are instructed to boldly claim victory through prayer.

IT IS WRITTEN:

"Call to Me, and I will answer you, and I will tell you great and mighty things which you do not know."

—JEREMIAH 33:3

"Whatever you ask in My name, I will do."

— JOHN 14:13-14

"Therefore I say, to you, whatever things you ask when you pray, believe that you receive them, and you will have them."

—MARK 11:24

Whatever you are facing, trust God with it. Ask Him to take away your anxieties, fears and feelings of frustration. When you trust the Lord, you will rest in His care.

"God knows that soldiers are to be made only in battle. They are not to be grown in peaceful times. We may grow the stuff of which soldiers are made; but warriors are really educated by the smell of gun powder, in the midst of whizzing bullets and roaring cannons. Is He not developing in you the qualities of a soldier by throwing you into the heat of battle, and should you not use every application to become a conqueror?"

—CHARLES SPURGEON

Prayer is the most powerful tool you have as a believer! It is your direct connection to our Heavenly Father. You can pray instantly, anytime, anyplace and for any reason.

Every person on this earth has a need. However, every person does not have a direct link to God to call on Him. God's ears are open to His children only and others, He will not hear.

In your prayer life, you receive help from the Holy Spirit. The Holy Spirit knows what things you need to petition God for. Whenever there is a problem, you can go directly to God in prayer. You do not have to wait for a specific time. God is always available to hear your request.

It is appropriate to ask God to show you how to listen to Him and how to hear His voice. After that, tell God you want to know more about Him. God wants this type of relationship with you. He wants to show you more of Himself every day. The more God reveals to you about Himself, the more you will want to know.

IT IS WRITTEN:

"For I desire mercy and not sacrifice, and the knowledge of God more than burnt offerings."
—HOSEA 6:6

"Cast all your anxiety on Him because He cares for you."
—1 PETER 5:7(NIV)

Remember, God is love, and He loves you and me. No matter what the problem, you must believe that God will work it out for your good.

IT IS WRITTEN:

"And we know that all things work together for good to those who love God, to those who are called according to His purpose."
—ROMANS 8:28

Here are six things I recommend you consider when praying:

1. Let your prayers flow from a heart filled with love, compassion, and forgiveness.
2. Recognize that your prayers are the link between a person's needs and God's inexhaustible resources.
3. Be sure to identify with the need of another person.
4. Always desire the highest good for the life of the person you are praying for.
5. Be willing to be part of the answer in meeting another person's needs.
6. Be willing to persevere.

Thoughts to meditate upon to Prepare for God's Abundant Life:

- Remember, there is power in prayer.
- God hears the prayers of His children.
- You honor God when you pray.
- Acknowledge God in all your ways, and He will direct your path.

Everything begins with God

The earth and the fullness thereof began with God. Man had his beginning with God. The Bible tells us that God is the Alfa and the Omega—the beginning and the end.

As a believer, your life starts with God. You should begin and end each day with God. He is the reason that you exist. With God, you can do all things. Without Him, you can do nothing.

Everything you do on a daily basis should be centered around God. And while tomorrow is not promised to anyone, God gave each of us a measure of faith.

God knows you will face many unknowns in your life. Always remember that He is in control and that He is a loving God—who simply asks that you love Him, abide in His Word, and have but a measure of faith in Him.

IT IS WRITTEN
---

*"If you have faith as a mustard seed, you will say
unto the mountain, move from here to there; and it will
move; and nothing will be impossible for you.*

—MATTHEW 17:20B

God designed man to need Him. That is why you can never be self-sufficient without Him. There are limitations that God has placed upon you.

God wants you to acknowledge Him always. This is a commandment of God. It is not a statement to be taken casually.

*"Trust in the Lord with all your heart, and lean not
on your own understanding; in all your ways acknowledge
Him, and He shall direct your paths".*

—PROVERBS 3: 5, 6

THOUGHTS TO MEDITATE UPON
TO PREPARE FOR GOD'S ABUNDANT LIFE:

- Begin everyday with God.
- Acknowledge God in everything you do.
- Look for God to help and guide you once you have acknowledged Him.

15

DILIGENCE AND WEALTH

"The plans of the diligent lead surely to plenty, but those of everyone who is hasty surely to poverty."

—PROVERBS 21:5

There is a price to pay for a dream, a vision, or a goal. Diligence is a price that must be paid. In order to get wealth God's way, you must be diligent in your work.

IT IS WRITTEN:

"He who has a slack hand becomes poor, but the hand of the diligent makes rich."
—PROVERBS 10:4

"The soul of a lazy man desires, and has nothing; but the soul of the diligent shall be made rich."
—PROVERBS 13:4

A diligent man is a satisfied man. The lazy man is always dreaming and wanting but never willing to pay the price of perseverance. Thus, he comes up to frustration and emptiness.

To be diligent is to continue to move forward at all times. Progress must be made to reach your goal. Sometime the progress may be a few inches, and other days, it will be more.

You should never worry about being off course when moving towards your goal. For example, I remember reading about Apollo Seven, the missile that carried several astronauts to the moon. It was said that 90% of the time, the missile was off course. However, corrections were made each time to bring the missile back on its course to reach the moon.

Remember, you should never let surrounding conditions dictate whether you work toward your goal or not. Your conditions to move ahead may never be perfect, so you must remain diligent and do something each day to move closer to your dream in spite of any conditions. There will always be something to do.

You must have a plan to do something each day that will bring you closer to your goal. Keep in mind, the best way to fight poverty is with a weapon loaded with diligence.

"Show me someone content with mediocrity, and I'll show you somebody destined to failure."

—JOHNETTA COLE

THOUGHTS TO MEDITATE UPON
TO PREPARE FOR GOD'S ABUNDANT LIFE:

- A vision, with a plan, prayer, and diligence will come true for you as a believer.
- Diligent hands will make one wealthy.
- Diligence and laziness are on the opposite side of the same coin.
- Remember, we must pay the price of always being diligent.

God is committed to your success

God wants each of His children to succeed because He planted a seed of desire within you. Each of you wants to achieve some form of success during your lifetime.

The Bible contains basic ideas for achieving genuine success. God has provided the knowledge for you to become successful according to His Word. He has given each of you the talents and gifts to be successful.

The Bible speaks of success as "prosperity." To prosper is to be successful in all good things you endeavor.

When God created man, He made us to be successful in all things. God made man to have successful rule over the earth and everything in it. In essence, God made man to be a god over the earth. God made man somewhat like Himself. God rules over everything. Man was supposed to rule over the earth.

IT IS WRITTEN:

Then God said, "Let Us make man in Our image, according to Our likeness; let them have dominion (rule) over the fish of the sea, over the birds of the air, and over the cattle, over all the earth and over every creeping thing that creeps on the earth."

— GENESIS 1:26

God has many promises for His children. There are over three hundred promises in the Bible. These promises are available to you—the believer, but with some conditions. If you are a disobedient believer, you may hinder receipt of God's promises to you.

THOUGHTS TO MEDITATE UPON
TO PREPARE FOR GOD'S ABUNDANT LIFE:

- We can be sure that God desires for the believer to succeed. He will never give up on us and we should never give up on ourselves.

- After we lay out our daily plans to succeed, we must follow them daily and God promises to direct our steps. (Proverbs 16:9)

- It is always best to ask God for wisdom in every endeavor, because it is wisdom that ultimately brings success.

- And remember, the Scriptures tell us that through Christ we can do all things.

Persistence throughout your life

"There is in this world no such force as the force of a man determined to rise. The human soul cannot be permanently chained."
— W. E. DuBois

Your most valuable asset can be your willingness to persist longer than anyone else can. There is one main common denominator that flows through the lives of every great person— persistence.

IT IS WRITTEN:

"I press toward the goal for the prize of the upward call of God in Christ Jesus."
— PHILIPPIANS 3:14

Napoleon Hill, in his book "Think and Grow Rich," records that he studied five hundred of the wealthiest men in the world and concluded that all of these men had one thing in common! They were all persistent.

Most people are good "starters," but poor finishers of most things they begin. People are prone to quitting at the first signs of defeat. "Old man failure" cannot cope with persistence.

I believe that "God's power" sustains the person who still fights on, even after the battle has been lost and everyone else has long since quit. I believe that persistence and a conviction of purpose are the main components in all achievements. Persistence is vital to success because defeats, failures, mistakes, and delays are inevitable. Persistence is required if you are going to overcome discouragement.

Your goal should be to stay committed to God. Remember it is God who will give you the ability to persist in your desires for success.

THOUGHTS TO MEDITATE UPON
TO PREPARE FOR GOD'S ABUNDANT LIFE:

- Stay the course.
- Always ask yourself, "What is the next step?" Then, take it.
- You may be closer to winning than you think, so keep forging ahead. By doing so, you demonstrate your faith in God and yourself.
- Every step forward brings you closer to your goal; therefore never give up.
- Remember God is with you all the way. This is faith in its truest form.

Facing burnout

IT IS WRITTEN:

*"Come to me, all you who labor and are heavy laden,
and I will give you rest."*
— MATTHEW 11:28

*"Take My yoke upon you and learn from Me, for I
am gentle and lowly in heart, and you will find rest for
your souls."For My yoke is easy and My burden is light."*
— MATTHEW 11:29-30

God loves you and wants to care for you. He wants to handle all of your needs and worries. God does not want you to run yourself into exhaustion by trying to do too much.

Too often, you can become consumed each day with household chores, business meetings, jobs, and careers. Your plate stays filled with overbooked appointments and scheduling, running from one meeting to another. You eat lunch on the go to make the next business deal across town, and are already twenty minutes late. You are constantly trying to jam a list of twenty things into an eight-hour time slot. You may sometimes feel you are nearing the end of your rope—approaching a "burnout" point.

Are you feeling any of these symptoms? Do you find yourself overly critical of others, blaming others for your behavior, expecting too much of yourself or others, feeling self-doubt, or questioning your drive for success? Are you feeling exhausted or tired more than usual?

A feeling of burnout usually comes after extended periods of exhaustion. This weary feeling seems to affect the body and mind. You will often allow disappointment to set in, and begin to feel that the world has not granted you all that you believe you should have.

Whenever you encounter days or periods like this, accompanied with feelings of sheer exhaustion, you should go before the Lord and claim His promise for renewed strength.

It is written:

"But those who wait on the Lord shall renew their strength; They shall mount up with wings like eagles. They shall run and not be weary; they shall walk and not faint."
— Isaiah 40:31

Remember the power and wisdom of God. He made your body; and surely understands how easy it is to become overextended and burned out. God knows how to strengthen you if you ask. It is during these times that it is important for you to return to the basics of life—reading the Bible, praying, abiding in God, and allowing God's Word to abide in you.

As a believer, you will sometimes go through periods of struggling with life issues and problems. When you seek God in hope of finding answers, you may feel that you do not always get an answer. You may believe that He is not there. But God is always there, observing your every step.

What is best for you to do when this occurs? You need to seek God earnestly and ask Him, "God what are You saying to me? What is it that You need for me to know?" Now you must wait for God to reveal to you what He desires to share with you.

Perhaps you should consider a time for daily devotional, and the reading of God's Word. Eventually, you will begin to respond to issues in your life in a godly way. You will begin to enjoy God's peace and His presence in your life. The love of God will permeate in your midst. You will begin to feel like you are on track again with Jesus, and will have a "sense of knowing," that God will do what He said, that He never fails, and that nothing is ever too hard for Him.

Thoughts to meditate upon to Prepare for God's Abundant Life:

- Meditate on God's Word to reap the benefits of peace and tranquility.
- Commit all of your daily doings to God and He will keep your heart and mind at peace.
- Focus daily on having a God "mind-set"
- Pray when you get the feeling of work or business overload!

16

WEALTH REQUIRES THINKING BIG

"I can do all things through Christ who strengthens me."

— PHILIPPIANS 4:13

The Bible did not say that we can do some things, or we can do small things. It says we can do all things.

Most people only feel comfortable doing small things. Perhaps it is because small thinking requires little faith, while big achievements and big goals require great faith. Maybe great faith is rare.

Consider a little scenario that may shed some light on thinking big. You are a child of God. Your playing small does not serve the world. There is nothing enlightening about shrinking in order for others to feel less insecure around you. We are all meant to shine, as children do. We were born to make manifest the "glory" of God that is within us. It is not just in some of us! It is in all of us. As we let our light shine, we unconsciously give other people permission to do the same.

As we are liberated from our own fears, our presence automatically liberates others.
— MARIONNE WILLIAMSON

Thinking small, leads to small results that lead to being broke and unfulfilled. Big thinking and big results lead to having both money and options.

Dream big! Only big dreams have the power to move your mind and spirit! One must come to realize that it requires no more effort to aim high in life than it does to aim low.

I believe that most people feel they do not deserve to live an abundant life. Contrary to what we believe, the Bible declares we can live an abundant life.

"I have come that they may have life, and that they may have it more abundantly."
— JOHN 10:10B

An old cliché says, "if it is to be, it is up to me." There is a host of truth in this statement, because God will not make your dreams come true. It is up to you to make your own dreams a reality, with the help of God.

I believe everything in life we desire—big or small—will come with degrees of challenges attached. In order to reach your goals in life, it will require perseverance and sacrifice.

How will you know if a vision or dream is obtainable? The answer is this, if you can honestly see yourself with the vision, you can attain it. God will not allow you to see the results in your mind if he did not intend for you to accomplish it.

An old cliché states, "whatever the mind of man can conceive and believe, he can achieve." God made you this way—you were made to do great things in life.

But, God must receive the glory for Himself in every achievement. Whether the achievement is large or small, it does not matter. God wants you to use your faith in everything that you do. If it is not by faith, God is not pleased.

"But without faith it is impossible to please Him."
— HEBREWS 11:6B

Could it be a form of selfishness to think small and get small results? With a small result, you are limited in your ability to help others. On the other hand, if you think big and get a much larger result, you can help others. Now you are a blessing to others and you will be rewarded by God for being a giver.

If your goal is to reach a certain financial status, think in terms of the number of people you can help when you have obtained your goal. If you have a business, there is nothing wrong with a desire to become a millionaire, but your motives must be pure in how you plan to use your gain.

I believe that if your motives consider the needs of the poor, then God will help you obtain your goals. When your motives are self-centered, God will not bless you abundantly.

It is written:

"Blessed is he who considers the poor; The Lord will deliver him in time of trouble. The Lord will preserve him and keep him alive, and he will be blessed on the earth."
— PSALM 41:1

Fear is another reason that millions of people live a meager lifestyle. The opposite of fear is confidence. Any great achievement requires confidence. No one is born into this world with a high degree of confidence. Confidence is an acquired mindset. One of the best ways to conquer fear is to take action. Action, action, and more action will eliminate all fear,

All people experience fear at times—the poor and the wealthy. However, the wealthy and poor perceive fear differently. The poor perceive fear, but often find no strength to move forward. The wealthy perceive fear, but move forward in spite of it.

People are measured by the size of their dreams. Visualize a big future and do not sell yourself short. Develop your blueprint for success.

THOUGHTS TO MEDITATE UPON
TO PREPARE FOR GOD'S ABUNDANT LIFE:

- Remember small thinking leads to small results, and big thinking leads to big results.
- God always applauds big thinking.
- Big thinking requires more faith than small thinking.
- Use your faith to create big goals to glorify God.

Facing adversities in your life

IT IS WRITTEN:

"I will be glad and rejoice in Your mercy. For You have considered my trouble; You have known my soul in adversities."

— PSALM 31:7

Adversity is one of life's inescapable experiences. God will use the trials you face to train you to be a strong, spirit-filled soldier for Jesus Christ.

Often God will not prevent adversity in your life in order to mold, prepare, and perfect you to serve Him. God cannot use you in your present state, so He prunes and shapes you throughout your lifetime, in hopes of perfecting you like His Son Jesus.

God does not delight in sending hardship or calamity into your life, but He will use trials and tribulations in a manner that will bring you into a state of repentance. Adversity is a bridge to a deeper relationship with God.

When you stay focused on God, He becomes your source for encouragement and spiritual uplift. He is your strength during periods of disappointment and adversity.

IT IS WRITTEN:

"For I know the thoughts that I think toward you, says the Lord, thoughts of peace and not evil, to give you a future and a hope."
—JEREMIAH 29:11

During periods of adversity, you must hold fast to God's Word. You must believe and know that God has many blessings in store for you, more than you can imagine. God holds your future in His hands, and you will never lose by looking forward to what He has planned for you.

IT IS WRITTEN:

"No eye has seen, no ear has heard, no mind has conceived, what God has prepared for those who love Him."
—1 CORINTHIANS 2:9

Remember, adversity is one of God's greatest tools for advancing spiritual growth. The way you respond will make all the difference. God has a purposeful response to any adversity you face. It fits His plan for your future. Just respond to the adversity in the right way. You may not understand exactly what God is doing, but you must trust Him. God is preparing you, as a believer, for what lies ahead.

It is written:

"For My thoughts are not your thoughts, Nor are your ways My ways, says the Lord. For as the heavens are higher than the earth, So are My ways higher than your ways, And My thoughts higher than your thoughts."

—Isaiah 55:8-9

Thoughts to meditate upon to Prepare for God's Abundant Life:

- Never allow yourself to become discouraged about anything.
- Consider all adversities as the investment needed for you to get stronger.
- Adversity is a part of succeeding.
- Adversity will shape your character; so it is good for you.

Facing your fears

Every human being on the face of this earth has a fear of something. Aside from the fear of falling or loud noises that we seem to have at birth, most of our fears are learned behaviors.

The unknown breeds fear. The more you learn about the subject you fear, the less fear it holds on you.

To overcome fear, act as if it is impossible to fail, and you will overcome fear. Do the things you fear, and the death of fear is certain. The Bible also says, "perfect love dissipates fear."

IT IS WRITTEN:

"For God has not given us a spirit of fear, but of power and of love and of a sound mind."
—2 TIMOTHY 1:7

"There is no fear in love; but perfect love casts out fear, because fear involves torment. But he who fears has not been made perfect in love. "
—1 JOHN 4:18

God can use the fear, frustration, and feelings of hopelessness you feel to bring you to closer to Him. Fear is an emotion that can be overcome by faith in God's Word. He wants you to live without fear.

The Devil wants you to live in fear. He knows that you cannot accomplish much when you live in a constant state of fear. Maintaining God's power and a sound mind will give you the ability to control fear and overcome the Devil's temptation.

Whenever you are experiencing fear as a child of God, you can claim His promises.

IT IS WRITTEN:

"The Lord is my helper; I will not fear, what man can do to me."
—HEBREWS 13:6

Through the years, I have found that the majority of my friends, family, business associates, and peers tend to experience many of the same basic fears. Most of them have all encountered or faced the fear of failure, poverty, criticism, ill health, loss of a loved one, old age, or death. Ironically, these fears are more often than not, based upon something unknown, and not yet experienced.

Life teaches you, however, that if you live long enough you will ultimately come face-to-face with one or more of these fears. It is your initial encounter with one or more of these fears that, as a believer, your eyes will be opened and you will gain the wisdom and understanding of God's love—you will begin to realize and know there is no need to fear the unknown for God will strengthen, love you, and ease your burden. You simply have to put it in God's hands. He will see you through.

IT IS WRITTEN:

"Fear not, for I am with you! Be not dismayed, for I am your God, I will strengthen you, and yes, I will help you. I will uphold you with my righteous right hand. "
—ISAIAH 41:10

THOUGHTS TO MEDITATE UPON
TO PREPARE FOR GOD'S ABUNDANT LIFE:

- The word fear stands for: false - emotions - appearing - real.
- Face your fears with God by your side, and your fears dissipate.
- Never consider fear — only faith.

Consider the poor

When you consider the poor—"the least of these", the disenfranchised, the underserved—God will bless you. For when you bless others with your goodness, mercy, and kindness, the Lord will continue to preserve you, bless you, protect you, sustain you on your sick bed, be merciful unto you, and keep you during your times of trouble and need.

IT IS WRITTEN:

"Blessed is he who considers the poor; The Lord will deliver him in time of trouble."
— PSALM 41:1

God's Word teaches you that you are to share your blessings with those in need. When God blesses you with prosperity, He expects you to help those who have a need.

The Bible says that you are to love others as you would love yourself. I believe that this is where many of God's children fall short. Ask yourself, "how many people do you know who love their neighbor as themselves?" Do you?

"But whoever has this world's goods and sees his brother in need, and shuts up his heart from him, how does the love of God abide in him?"

— 1 John 3:17

"Jesus said to him, 'You shall love the Lord your God with all your heart, with all your soul, and with all your mind.' This is the first and great commandment, And the second is like it; You shall love your neighbor as yourself."

—Matthew 22:37-39

As a believer, you may not see enough evidence of this commandment throughout the world. In fact, you see just the opposite. There is too much poverty, hate, and illness throughout the world, and not enough caring, sharing, and love.

God himself is love, and He desires for us to imitate Him. That means that each of us should love and care for one another, as we would love and care for ourselves.

Thoughts to meditate upon
to Prepare for God's Abundant Life:

- God blesses us to be a blessing to others.
- We honor God by helping the less fortunate.
- The Bible says we are our brother's keeper.

17

ooooo

STRENGTH IN CHARACTER AND WEALTH

"We have joy with our troubles, because we know that these troubles produce patience, and patience produces character, and character produces hope."

—ROMANS 5:3-4

The number one quality of character is truthfulness. Always be honest and objective with yourself. Personal courage is the hallmark of great character and achievement. True character exhibits integrity through consistent moral excellence.

"The collapse of character begins with compromise."
—Frederick Douglas

Do you realize that your character is developed somewhat like a diamond? A true diamond begins as a common carbon. But over time with constant pressure, something of rare value is created. As a believer, your character is developed over time through the suffering that God uses to purify the diamond within you.

"Character is the sum total of all of our habits."
—Unknown

If a man has built a "sound character," it makes but little difference what people say about him, because he will win at the end.
—Napoleon Hill

God desires to manifest "His character" through your personality, and giftedness. When you allow the Holy Spirit to work within you, you become a vessel of His love in action. You imitate Jesus by reflecting His compassion, love, and mercy to others. You bring glory to God when you serve others.

In other words, your character must be changed in order to be more like Jesus. God's ultimate desire is for you to acquire and demonstrate the "character of Christ." To be of great character, you should strive to embody qualities such as patience, empathy, hospitability, generosity, prayerfulness, and to be a true servant of God.

"Of all the qualities necessary for success, none comes before character."
—Ernesta Procope

"Strive to make something of yourselves, then strive to make the most of yourselves."
—ALEXANDER CRUMMELL

The character of the believer must be impeccable at all times. Dishonesty does not fit in the life of a child of God. If you do something dishonest, you are essentially tossing a boomerang. Good comes from good acts, just as certainly as bad comes from bad acts. Each act is an unfailing boomerang.

THOUGHTS TO MEDITATE UPON
TO PREPARE FOR GOD'S ABUNDANT LIFE:

- Our character makes way to our success.
- Our character is a result of our habits.
- Our name plus our character tells more of who we are.
- We rise or fall in life depending upon our character.

Facing failure in your life

Too many people hesitate to start a business or other venture because of the possibility of failure. While every human being may face some degree of temporary defeat or setback, and in some cases even failure, this does not mean you have failed. It simply means, that you may need to experience setbacks and some temporary defeat in order to attain your true success, if you learn from it.

"Most great people have attained their greatest success just one step beyond their greatest failure."
—Napoleon Hill

God will sometimes allow you to experience temporary defeat in order to teach you an important lesson. When you are in relationship with God, and learn to listen to His voice, He may direct you another way.

As a result, you will grow in the right direction because of your spiritual connection. You will become wiser, and better able to discern what will or will not work. You will be better able to teach others what works.

When your mind is completely fixed on God, He will lead you along a path where most setbacks are eliminated. You do not always have to experience setbacks or defeat.

God will lead you when you depend on Him. He said in His Word, "He would never leave us or forsake us."

As a youngster, I attended a circus that featured members of the Flying Wallenda Family. I was amazed at their ability to continue performing high wire feats given the tragedies they had faced over time. Why were they not afraid of falling—a failure that could result in another tragic death?

I found my answer when reading an article on the thoughts of Toni Wallenda, grandchild of the great Karl Wallenda:

> **A Fixed Point** - When I was seven years old, my grandfather, Karl Wallenda, put me on a wire two feet off the ground. He taught me all the elementary skills: how to hold my body so that I remained stiff and rigid; how to place my feet on the wire with my big toe on the wire and my heel to the inside; how to hold the pole with my elbows close to my body. But the most important thing that my grandfather taught me was that I needed to focus my attention on a point at the other end of the wire. I need a point to concentrate

on to keep me balanced.

The ultimate focus on my life is Jesus Christ. The Bible says that we need to focus our eyes on a fixed point, we need to fix our eyes on Jesus, the Author and Perfector of our faith (Hebrews 12:2). I learned that and made it part of my life more than 25 years ago.

Confidence in Our Father - At one time or another I have taken each of my four children—Alida, Andrea, Aurelia and Alessandro—on my shoulders as I have walked across the wire. In those situations, the children really can't do any balancing; I'm the one who has to balance and support them.

People have asked them, "Aren't you scared?"

"No," they have said.

And when they have been asked, "Why aren't you scared?" They have answered, "Because that's my daddy." They have confidence in me because I'm their daddy.

And I have confidence in my heavenly Father. I know that He will take me all the way across this Chasm of Life until I meet Him face to face. (ToniWallenda)

Like the Wallendas, you should be prepared to continue with your life, your goals and objectives in spite of failures or tragedies. Learn and grow from the strength you get from God. Get ready for the next venture.

It is ok to reflect on the reason for the setback, but continue to move ahead. You should never focus on failure, but focus on God. Meditate on God's Word and listen to the "small voice" within for instruction. If you listen intently to God, sometimes it will make the difference between your success and failure, joy and sorrow, pleasure and pain.

You must always say to yourself, "I will never accept defeat."

Every prominent person has endured setbacks such as hearing "no" more often than "yes." The secret to success is not the avoidance of defeat, rather the growth through defeat. A loss is always a potential lesson. There is not one of you who learned to walk without falling first and falling many times before walking.

Everyone makes mistakes. Losses are inevitable. The main question is, "Did you learn from your mistake?" After each defeat you must ask, "What went wrong and how can I prevent it from happening again?"

"Lack of self-confidence and the fear of failure are opposite sides of the same coin."
—Charles Johnson

"I am not afraid of failing."
—Michael Jordan

"The only thing worse than failing is being afraid to try."
—Frank Mingo

Remember, failure is not final!

Thoughts to meditate upon to Prepare for God's Abundant Life:

- Never ever consider failing! Failure is not an option!
- Think only of succeeding.
- Visualize your success and ask God to help you. He desires for you to succeed.

Prosperity is your right

Apart from God, you cannot achieve prosperity. You may labor, plan, due diligence with wisdom and vitality, but God is the source of all blessings. He is the foundation of life, health, food and everything else you need for prosperity.

IT IS WRITTEN:

"Beloved I pray that you may prosper in all things,
and be in health, just as your soul prospers."

— 3 JOHN 2

It is God's desire that you prosper in every way. There are over three hundred promises in the Bible, and many of these promises ensure the health, wealth, and welfare of you, the believer.

As a believer, you should not accept living in a state of lack. This is not scriptural. The Bible promises just the opposite.

IT IS WRITTEN:

"I come that you may have life and have it more
abundantly."

—JOHN 10:10

The Bible tells you that God will never change. His Word will always be the same. This says that you can always rely on God.

God does not desire the Devil's children to live a more abundant life than His own. Even though it may appear at times that the Devil's children have great abundance, do not be deceived. God will not be mocked. You may be observing a temporary lifestyle of the unbeliever. Only God knows the extent of the prosperity of the unbeliever.

Know that it is God's plan for you to be successful and prosperous! Does this mean that you can just sit down and do nothing but wait for God to drop money from heaven? No! You must pursue your vision, write it down, and take action to pursue prosperity with your faith in God. There is no free lunch, even in God's kingdom. Every believer must pay a price for any achievement, whether it is large or small.

God gave each believer the essentials to be prosperous. God gave you a wonderful body, an awesome brain, along with His powerful promises. In return, He asks that you strive to live your life according to the Ten Commandments. You will be richly blessed when you are obedient. On the other hand, you may not be as blessed if you are disobedient.

Stop for a moment to reflect on just one awesome thing that God gave you—"your mind." Realize that you should have no excuse for not achieving anything you desire in life.

The human mind is one of God's greatest creations. No scientist can place the mind under any microscope and determine its capability or power. I truly believe that one single mind has the power to change the world!

With the help of God, there is no limit to what the mind of man can do!

IT IS WRITTEN:

"Most assuredly, I say to you, he who believes in Me, the works that I do he will do also; and greater works than these he will do, because I go to My Father."
—JOHN 14:12

All life is a gift from God.

It is written:

"Every good gift and every perfect gift is from above, and comes down from the Father of lights, with Whom there is no variation or shadow of turning."

—James 1:17

Thoughts to meditate upon
to Prepare for God's Abundant Life:

- Prosperity and poverty are in the power of the believer's words.
- The Bible tells us "we shall have what we say."
- Our prosperity also depends on our knowledge and belief in God's promises.
- God intended for His children to have prosperity.

The boldness in you

As a believer, you have been given boldness through the Word of God that allows you to speak with confidence. There is no reason for you to be shy and reserve, when it is clear that the Holy Spirit lives inside of you. The shed blood of Jesus gives you the right to be righteous. Once you are righteous, you can also be bold.

Keep in mind, however, there is a difference between boldness and arrogance. Arrogance is a display of pride, while boldness shows courage. A sense of great boldness is necessary to do great things in life for God's sake, such as stepping up to help feed hungry children in foreign places.

When you know that you can get God's help, you should have a sense of boldness about your request. In general, the believer can accomplish more by being bold as opposed to being reserve throughout your life.

God's Word tells you to approach the throne of God boldly. Jesus' death on the cross, made this possible. Your speech or appeal to God should be laced with love. Love should be the underlying motivation for your appeal or prayer, but boldness should be the overall inflection of the tone. Think boldness until it becomes a habit.

Boldness should be a way of life for you as a believer. "As a man thinks, so is he," is what the Scriptures tell us. Life will more often give in, to the person who is bold, as opposed to the person who lacks confidence.

Thoughts to meditate upon
to Prepare for God's Abundant Life:

- Be bold in everything you do.
- There are rewards in using discretionary boldness.
- God wants His children to approach His throne of grace with boldness.
- We are God's children; therefore, we have a right to be bold.

18

ooooo

Wealth and Leadership

"God sent Moses to Pharaoh to lead the children of Israel out of Egypt."

—Exodus 3:10

A leader is a person who can influence the behavior of other people—a people person. Reading is one of the qualities a leader uses to stay abreast of information. All leaders must lead with good up-to-date information. So why not look to the God for your strength, guidance, and decision making as a leader.

Leaders are also winners; and this is one of the reasons others will follow you. A leader is able to be out front leading the pact because he has confidence.

"This world is filled with followers, supervisors, and managers, but very few leaders."
—Miles Monroe

A leader at one time was a good follower. Not all good followers make good leaders. I believe a good leader understands the importance of relationships in any organization. A leader should be pushing forward at all times. He should be focusing on improving daily.

A leader who depends on God to lead Him will be a more effective leader. Followers will soon find out whether the leader truly cares about the people in the group.

As a leader, I believe you should never manage your team. Instead, you should learn to lead your team and manage yourself.

Your character as a leader, will always be under scrutiny by your followers. Thus, you must be worthy of your follower's trust. The quality of your leadership will be defined by your ability to get and keep followers.

Good leaders will usually possess certain qualities that affect their ability to lead others. The qualities of a good leader most likely include the ability to:

- Project a positive attitude at all times.
- Work well with a group or team.

- Resolve conflicts positively.

- Remain neutral, and accepting of input, criticism, etc.

- Serve as a good role model.

- Be a people person.

- Effectively communicate with others.

- Seek new ideas or opportunities, and ways to improve efficiency and effectiveness within the team, group, or organization.

How many of these qualities do you possess? If you are not sure, solicit feedback from your friends, family, or peers.

As a leader, you must be out front of the group making things happen. You must have a winner's attitude, and demonstrate that everyone in the group can win. You must strongly believe in the vision of the organization, and inspire the group to give their best. If you are to be a great leader, you will know how to bring out the best in each follower because you have learned how to bring out the best in yourself.

To be an effective leader, you should be reliable and consistent; and keep in mind that some followers may feel insecure and need encouragement. You must have confidence in yourself, and build confidence in others.

IT IS WRITTEN:

"Then Jesus said to them, 'Follow Me, and I will make you fishers of men."
—MATTHEW 4:19

Another great leadership quality is learning to treat others, as you want to be treated. It is good to stay balanced with everyone on the team by trading minds with the person you are trying to influence. As you lead, you should lift up the name of Jesus bringing your followers into the realm of God.

"You are the salt of the earth ...You are the light of the world...Let your light so shine before men, that they may see your good works and glorify your Father in heaven."
—Matthew 5: 13-16

As a leader, you should always strive to:

- Use your heart when dealing with a group.
- Give others the benefit of the doubt.
- Know when to back down.
- Not over react to conflict.
- Be an encourager.
- Always keep your word. Integrity is the most valuable and respected quality of leadership.

"No man can become a great leader of men unless He has a degree of human kindness in his own heart, and leads by suggestion and kindness, rather than by force."
—Unknown

Remember, as a believer, "you can do all things through Christ who gives you strength." Believe that you will be a better leader if you keep God's commandments, and keep God's Words in your heart, soul, spirit, and thinking. Know that nothing will bring you success as a leader without your belief in God's promises.

"Leaders are men who stand in the face of adversity, and men and women who are willing to continue the struggle no matter how uncomfortable or challenging."
—Unknown

THOUGHTS TO MEDITATE UPON
TO PREPARE FOR GOD'S ABUNDANT LIFE:

- Leaders are believers who create ways to move their team forward.
- The main repertoire of a believer is first being an example to your followers.
- A good leader stays informed.
- A leader must be sensitive to the growth and needs of your followers.

Trusting in God

Perhaps one of the most significant areas of my Christian walk has been learning to "trust God," especially in my career as a real estate professional. As a real estate professional, I would invest in a single family home, repair the home, and seek a buyer. It never entered my mind at that time to trust in God for the right buyer. I just did what other sellers did—simply ran an ad, distributed, and posted flyers.

Later in life, I learned to "trust" God and ask Him to help me find the right buyer who needed the house I wanted to sell. I took some risks while investing in real estate, and became quite successful. This was only possible, however, because of God's help. As I recall, I purchased nine houses and made approximately $20,000 profit per house (or $ 180,000) back in 1997. With each investment, I called on God to help find the right deal—one that would be affordable and beneficial to both buyer, and seller. After completing the repairs and renovations, I trusted God to help find the right buyer—a family or owner that was in need of good value for their investment.

It is written:

"But he who trusts in the Lord will be prospered."
—Proverbs 29:25b

I am grateful to God for allowing me to begin building wealth in 1997 because of the vision He gave me to enter real estate. Because of my initial success, I began to share my insight into real estate investing with other real estate professionals. By sharing my real estate skills with others, I was able to honor God by giving something back to the community.

Investing in real estate was fun and rewarding. It required faith and some risks. It was rewarding to see many of my real estate students buy and sell properties.

Through the years, I have come to realize that the most important factor in my success in the real estate industry was in fact—keeping God first, and ever present in my business negotiations, decision making, investments, and outcomes. I call it my "faith and trust" in God factor. I know that without God, I can do nothing. He is the source of all my wealth. He alone gave me the power to get wealth—financially, personally, mentally, and physically. God is good!

It is written:

"The blessing of the Lord makes one rich, and He adds no sorrow with it."
—Proverbs 10:22

It is amazing what you can accomplish when you acknowledge God in all aspects of your life. I received a call from a builder who wanted to sell a strip plaza to me that was valued at $700.000. I had never invested in a commercial property before. I initially told him that I was not interested, but the seller continued to call me at least once a month.

The truth of the matter was I was somewhat fearful of a purchase of that size. I had never invested in a property over $120,000. As I think back, there was some lack of faith on my part when the seller first called me about buying the property, because I could not see myself profiting from this investment. However, I did some soul searching and some figuring to see how viable this deal would be to me.

Approximately two weeks later, I decided to make an offer on the strip plaza. I made an offer of $360,000 to buy the property. I had a down payment of $25,000, and asked for 3% interest rate, seller financing, and a term of 15 years to pay off the loan. To my surprise, the seller accepted the offer!

The day after the closing, I began to do the repairs on the building with the help of a "handyman." From the day I made the initial investment to the day I sold the property, I kept God in the forefront—I asked Him constantly for guidance and reassurance that I was doing what He wanted.

Seven months later, I sold the building for $625,000. The buyers paid cash for the purchase which eliminated the need for a loan! I knew immediately that God had made that sale possible, because the buyers had been the first to come by to see the property.

This poem is befitting of the mindset I maintained throughout this venture:

I bargained for Life for a penny
And Life would pay no more,
However, I begged at evening
When I counted my scanty store;
For Life is just an employer,
He gives you what you ask,
But once you have set the wages,
Why, you must bear the task.
I worked for a menial's hire
Only to learn, dismayed,

That any wage I had asked of Life,
Life would have gladly paid.
—Jessie Belle Rittenhouse (1869–1948)

If you are facing a difficult challenge today, trust God with it. Say something like, "God, I trust You in this situation. I know that You are with me because Your Word says that You will always be with me and You will never leave me alone."

Ask God to remove any anxieties, fears, and feelings of frustration. After you have done this, you must have faith that He will help you. Next, watch Him work in your behalf. If you read this poem again (with God in the equation as your employer) and consider a "penny" relative to everything, you desire in life, you will see how well it works.

It is written:

"Trust in the Lord with all your heart, and lean not
on your own understanding; in all your ways acknowledge
Him, and He will direct your path."
— Proverbs 3:5-6

In my walk with God, there have been times in my life when some things did not make sense. The results that I had hoped for in certain situations did not happen. The outcome was much unexpected. I later discovered that God was leading me on another course of action. Then it occurred to me, that God knew what was best. His thoughts are higher than my thoughts, and He knows the future. Therefore, His ways will always be better than my ways.

THOUGHTS TO MEDITATE UPON
TO PREPARE FOR GOD'S ABUNDANT LIFE:

- In all that you do, rely on God. Know that He will direct your path.

- Know exactly what you want. Write your vision down. Set goals for attainment.

- See yourself already in possession of your dreams.

- Above all else, take action. Remember to ask God for His wisdom, and guidance for each and every step you take along the path towards attaining your dreams, and goals in life.

Your purpose in life

Purpose is about becoming what God created you to be and doing what God called you to do. The establishment of a clear central purpose or goal in life is the starting point of all success. Understanding your purpose in life, gives you something to live for. You have a reason to be excited.

A believer with a purpose spends more time in prayer. Because you are in the family of God, you can rely on God to help you. You will know the power that is released for you through prayer.

You must believe that God will answer your prayer. Because you are a believer, you must never doubt Him. You will attain a powerful position once you have prayed to God. You should be bold and ready to risk reaching for the stars, because you have a special relationship with God.

IT IS WRITTEN:
---

*"You will keep him in perfect peace, whose mind is
stayed on You, because he trusts in You."*
—ISAIAH 26:3

One of the most important thoughts that you must maintain daily is
your "purpose-driven thought" that is used to carry you to any height that
you can imagine. The greatest tragedy you could ever experience is not
death, but to live a life without purpose. God's main purpose in your life
is to glorify Him, and He will use any means necessary to accomplish this.

*"We must all find our true purpose like Michelangelo or Mozart
or Leonardo de Vinci. Each of us must develop a mission in life."*
—MICHAEL JACKSON

THOUGHTS TO MEDITATE UPON
TO PREPARE FOR GOD'S ABUNDANT LIFE:

- You must believe that you were placed here on earth for a
  purpose.
- There is power in pursuing your purpose.
- If you have purpose, you have life.
- Purpose adds value to life.

Facing obstacles in life

Obstacles are what you see when you take your eyes off God. Difficulties come not to obstruct, but to offer a clue that there is a better way. Spend your time focusing on the opportunities of tomorrow rather than the problems of today.

IT IS WRITTEN:

"What then shall we say to these things? If God is for us, who can be against us?"

—ROMANS 8:31

There will be times in your life when you face obstacles that may seem overwhelming. During these times, you may often feel that you have reached your lowest and weakest point. But God is always faithful in keeping His promises, and He will never leave you. His Word is His bond. His Word is all you need in trying times. When you are weak, He is strong. There is no problem too big for God to handle.

When Moses and the Israelites were trapped at the Red Sea, with Pharaoh and his army upon them and nowhere to go, there was no one to turn to but God. God allowed this impasse, so that His power would prevail as the Supreme power over the Devil.

Similarly, you will often encounter problems that make you feel helpless and powerless. Just like Moses, when you feel there is no place to go and no one to turn to, God will show you His love and power to help you.

Whenever you are faced with obstacles, speak God's Word!

IT IS WRITTEN:

"I can do all things through Christ who strengthens me."
—PHILIPPIANS 4:13

"I know that God is with me in this situation."
—HEBREWS 13:5

"Father God I thank you that He Who is in me is greater than he that is in the world."
—1 JOHN 4:4

"If God is for me, who can be against me?"
—ROMANS 8:31

"God is able to do exceedingly abundantly above all that I ask or think."
—EPHESIANS 3:20

"With man this is impossible, but with God all things are possible."
—MARK 10:27

THOUGHTS TO MEDITATE UPON
TO PREPARE FOR GOD'S ABUNDANT LIFE:

- You have the power of prayer when you face an obstacle.
- You can speak God's Word over the circumstances you face and ask for a change.
- Always rely on God to help you when there is an obstacle.

19

WEALTH AND GOD'S PROMISES TO YOU

"But thou shalt remember the LORD thy God: for it is He that giveth thee power to get wealth, that He may establish His covenant which He sware unto thy fathers, as it is this day."

—DEUTERONOMY 8:18

There are over three hundred promises in the Bible for God's children. There are a multitude of what I call "success promises" that God has committed to those who abide in Him.

God has promised to:

> *"Never leave or forsake us."*
>
> —Hebrews 13:5

> *"This Book of the Law shall not depart from your mouth, but you shall meditate in it day and night, that you may observe to do according to all that is written in it. For then you will make your way prosperous, and then you will have good success."*
>
> —Joshua 1:8

> *"Then you will prosper, if you take care to fulfill the statutes and judgments with which the Lord charged Moses concerning Israel. Be strong and of good courage; do not fear nor be dismayed."*
>
> —1 Chronicles 22:13

> *"So I answered them, and said to them, 'The God of heaven Himself will prosper us; therefore we His servants will arise and build, but you have no heritage or right or memorial in Jerusalem."*
>
> —Nehemiah 2:20

> *"And keep the charge of the Lord your God; to walk in His ways, to keep His statutes, His Commandments, His judgments, and His testimonies, as it is written in the Law of Moses, that you may prosper in all that you do and wherever you turn."*
>
> —1 Kings 2:3

"The Lord repay your work and a full reward be given you by the Lord God of Israel, under whose wings you have come for refuge."

—Ruth 2:12

"Delight yourself in the Lord and He will give you the desires of your heart."

—Psalm 37:4(niv)

"If anyone's work which He has built on it endures, He will receive a reward."

—1 Corinthians 3:14

"The Lord makes poor and makes rich; He brings low and lifts up."

—1 Samuel 2:7

It is God who gives wealth and it is God who can take it away. God is our Heavenly Father. For He says to Moses, "I will have mercy on whomever I will have mercy and I will have compassion on whomever I will have compassion." (Romans 9:15)

Thoughts to meditate upon
to Prepare for God's Abundant Life:

- Memorize one or two promises of God and stand on them.
- Remember, God's promises are His Word to the believer. Count on them.
- God's promises are good news to us.

Facing hardships in your life

Many times God will allow you to face hopeless circumstances in order to test your faith. The hopelessness forces you to seek God. It is then that you will find strength and refreshment.

Whenever a hardship blindsides you say, "God, I trust You in this situation. I know that 'all things work together for good for those who love God and are called according to His purpose.' (Romans 8:28) No matter what trials and tests come your way, know and say, "God is in control."

God will, in some cases, cause a hardship to come your way in order to teach you to use your faith. Each time you use your faith, it grows, and gets stronger. It is pleasing to God when you put your faith in Him.

IT IS WRITTEN:

"But without faith it is impossible to please Him, for he who comes to God must believe that He is, and that He is a rewarder of those who diligently seek Him."
— HEBREWS 11:6

When God wants to get your attention, He may place various trials and tribulations before you. When this occurs, pray this prayer:

To, You O Lord, I lift up my soul;
in You I trust, O my God
Do not let me be put to shame,
nor let my enemies triumph over me.
No one whose hope is in You
will ever be put to shame,
but they will be put to shame
who are treacherous without excuse.
Show me Your ways, O Lord,
teach me Your paths;

188

guide me in Your truth ad teach me,
for You are God my Savior,
and my hope is in You all day long.
— Psalm 25:1-5(NIV)

Remember, suffering may be part of life. It can be vital to your walk and service to Jesus Christ. It is not to be feared, but to be embraced. As a believer, you should feel hope and joy when you are willing to suffer as Jesus suffered.

It is written:

"But rejoice that you participate in the sufferings of Christ, so that you may be overjoyed when His glory is revealed."
— 1 Peter 4:13

Thoughts to meditate upon to Prepare for God's Abundant Life:

- Remember, hardships in life can sometimes become struggles.
- If nothing else, overcoming struggles can make you stronger.
- If you tend to add value to that for which you have struggled, look at the struggle as an investment in your future.

Facing disappointments in life

You will always face disappointing days in your life. How you handle your disappointments is what will be important in your life.

God will sometimes use disappointments in your life to bring you closer to Him. He wants you to depend on Him; therefore, He will use disappointments to improve your relationship with Him.

Disappointments are inevitable, but discouragement is a choice you make. Winners will tend to believe that disappointments come and go, just like tidal waves come and go.

Remember not to focus on your disappointments. When you focus on disappointing thoughts, other disappointing thoughts will be attracted.

Thoughts to meditate upon
to Prepare for God's Abundant Life:

- When facing disappointments, affirm to the Lord that, "He is my refuge and my fortress; my God in Him I will trust." (Psalm 91:2)

- Remember that the Bible tells you, "All things work together for good to those who love the Lord and who are called according to His purpose." (Romans 8:28)

- Do not focus on your disappointments for God promises that He will never leave you. He is always with you.

20

GOD'S COMMITMENT TO YOUR SUCCESS

"If you abide in Me, and My Word abides in you,
you can ask anything and it shall be done unto you."

— JOHN 15:7

Montel Williams once said, "There is nothing mystical about success. It's the ability to stay mentally locked in." I would add that the important element here is to stay mentally focused on what God would have you do.

Success is assured when we place our full dependence on God. This is a true promise of God. Our relationship with God will assure the success we strive for each day.

> "But thou shalt remember the LORD thy God: for
> it is He that giveth thee power to get wealth, that He may
> establish His covenant which He sware unto thy fathers,
> as it is this day. And it shall be, if thou do at all forget
> the LORD thy God, and walk after other gods, and serve
> them, and worship them, I testify against you this day
> that ye shall surely perish. As the nations which the LORD
> destroyeth before your face, so shall ye perish; because ye
> would not be obedient unto the voice of the LORD your
> God."
> —Deuteronomy 8: 18-20

When you surrender your life to God, you will have the power of God working within you during any situation. You will have a big advantage because your trust is in God and not man. God tells you never to depend on man, but to put all your trust in Him.

When God made you, He gave you the potential to do many great things and achieve great accomplishments. However, God placed you in a vacuum whose void can only be filled when you develop a relationship with Him. Without God, you can only exist to a certain extent. You will never truly find contentment, joy, and fulfillment in life without Him.

Attaining success is to love God with all your mind, soul, and strength. Once you do this, God will unlock the potential He has already placed inside of you. You were made with a great potential for success.

God gives you the opportunity to seek and develop a daily relationship with Him. If you think that you do not need God, His Word will remind you that "without Him, we can do nothing."(John 15:5) In order for you to be assured of success, it is important to follow His rules.

IT IS WRITTEN:

"The Lord said to Joshua, always remember what is written in the Book the teachings. Study it day and night to be sure to obey everything that is written there. If you do this, you will be wise and successful in everything. "
—JOSHUA 1:8

God desires that you place Him first in your heart. But, His presence and position in your heart is up to you. You must invite Him to dwell within you.

IT IS WRITTEN:

"Though I stand at the door of man's heart and knock. If anyone hears My voice and opens the door. I will come in to him and dine with him, and he with Me."
—REVELATION 3:20

God desires that all of His children attain the success they desire. He gave each of you the potential for success when He created you. You must ask God for His help and work diligently to progress toward your predetermined goals.

Success is not luck. It will only come as a result of your relationship with God. The success you attain depends solely on God—not yourself or anyone else. You must remember that only God knows what He has planned for you. All success is predicated on future occurrences. As you depend on God, He will direct you according to His will, power and knowledge of the future.

If you had the option of choosing a human business partner or God as your business partner, who would you choose? Do you see where I am going with this rhetorical question? Is there anything that God does not know?

There is success in God. There is success in His wisdom. Wisdom always comes before any degree of success. Wisdom is a higher degree of understanding.

It is written:

"In all thy getting, get understanding."
—Proverbs 4:7

God contains all wisdom. All wisdom flows from God. Before the earth was created, God had wisdom. When you ask God for wisdom, you are in essence asking for success. God knows you need His wisdom to succeed in life.

You must believe that He will give you wisdom. You cannot doubt Him. Once you ask for His wisdom, you must believe that you already have it. This is faith in its truest form.

God will make you wait at times before achieving large goals and big dreams. Most of the time when God asks you to wait for success, it is because He knows that you are not ready.

Success does not merely depend on how well you do the things you enjoy, but it also depends on how conscientiously you perform those duties you do not enjoy. I have discovered that sometimes success comes by doing those things you may not always like, because they are things that will help you grow in spirit and expertise.

IT IS WRITTEN:

"The Lord has pleasure in the prosperity of His servant."

—PSALM 35:27

To assure success God's way, you must:

- Be a child of God.

- Live a life that is pleasing to God.

- Keep His commandments.

- Trust in Him.

- Rely on Him.

- Make Him first in your life.

Remember, God knows all the roads that lead to success. However, you must connect with Him in a relationship and remain connected to Him in order to have your prayers answered.

Success requires a heart-and-soul effort. You will only put your heart and soul into something you desire. As you press forward to succeed, set goals, deadlines, and target dates. You will only accomplish that which you plan to accomplish.

IT IS WRITTEN:

"Beloved, I pray that you may prosper in all things and be in health just as your soul prospers."

— 3 JOHN 2

Remember, there is no success without sacrifice, and sacrificing means investing. When you give up something today, you will gain more for tomorrow.

"To get profit without risk, experience without danger, and reward without work is as impossible as it is to live without being born."
—A.P. SOUTHEY

Success always begins as a thought. You must imagine yourself as being successful. When you do, your body and mind moves in the direction of that success. An imaginary scene takes place in the mind that is real to the brain, as if this is actually happening. Over time, your body and thoughts spontaneously react in a positive way until a successful way is created. Ultimately, your outer world will reflect the scene that your inner world has created.

If you can imagine success, your mind will set up mental pictures that are connected with the image that you are holding in your mind. You are in essence giving your mind an order of the success you desire and it is the job of the brain to bring it into reality.

The opposite is true if you imagine failure. Your mind will create pictures of oppositions, setbacks, and failures. As a result, you will experience your desired reflection of failure in the outer world. Remember, what you see and imagine in your mind, will be reflected in your world.

This is true for all people. Your outer world is where you live. How you choose to live will be reflected by the thoughts rooted in your mind as a seed once planted or imagined.

"The secret of success is to learn to accept the impossible, to do without the indispensable, and to bear the intolerable."
— Nelson Mandela

"It's not a question of can you succeed; a better question is will you succeed?"
— George Johnson

Remember; it has been said that the person who never had a chance, never took one. Success is never won by chance or luck, but by choice.

God wants all of His children to succeed. First, He planted a seed of desire for success in each one of you. Every human being desires some form of success.

The Bible contains many principles of genuine success for everyone. This tells me that God has made the knowledge of how to be successful available in His Word. He has given each of us talents and gifts, that when developed and employed can yield success in our lives.

The Bible speaks of success as "prosperity." They are both the same. To prosper is to be successful.

When God created you, He made you to be successful in all things. God created you to prosper on the earth, and enjoy an abundance of everything on it. In essence, God made you to be a god on the earth.

God made man somewhat like Himself. Although Satan is illegally ruling on earth, God intended for man to have rule on earth, just as He has rule over all.

IT IS WRITTEN:

"Then God said, 'Let Us make man in Our image, according to Our likeness; let them have dominion (rule) over the fish of the sea, over the birds of the air, and over the cattle, over all the earth and over every creeping thing that creeps on the earth."
—GENESIS 1:26

"Now is the judgment of this world; now the ruler (Devil) of this world will be cast out."
—JOHN 12:31

Thoughts to meditate upon
to Prepare for God's Abundant Life:

- Know that God desires for you to succeed. He will never give up on you. You should never give up on yourself.

- Lay out your daily plans to succeed, and follow them. God promises to direct your steps.

- Ask God for wisdom in every endeavor, because it is wisdom that ultimately brings success.

- Remember the Scriptures tell us that through Christ we can do all things.

- The primary secret for attaining success is to have God in your life.

Self-control in your life

Every sin in the life of the believer can be attributed to a lack of self-control. You must learn how to rule over your emotions rather than let your emotions rule over you. Feelings are just emotions. You should never pursue or make decisions about anything based solely on your feelings or emotions. Since your feelings can be misleading and unreliable, you should base all of your decisions and actions on the Word and the promises of God.

The Bible does not talk about relying on your feelings. But instead, it reminds you to rely on God and His promises. Sadly, too many people make decisions based solely on feelings and emotions.

Your feelings and emotions are detected and influenced by your frame of mind. Feelings come and go. Do not work on your goal simply when you feel like working. You must take charge of your emotions. Do not waste energy on disappointment, anger, and bitterness. Take control of all your feelings. Be quick to forgive anyone who has mistreated you. Do not waste time with slothfulness or idleness, for these traits work against your ability to reach your goal in a timely manner.

To be a believer with self-control and the power of God in your life, is a powerful combination. You will be equipped to accomplish great things.

Self-control covers a multitude of things that are necessary to reach goals and make dreams come true. Self-control entails having your body and mind work as one.

Once you are able to control yourself, you can control your ability to attain success in your life. You will have the ability to control what you focus on, and will be able to keep your thoughts directed on the necessary and important things that will bring you success.

"A man is what he thinks about all day long."
— UNKNOWN

IT IS WRITTEN:

"As a man thinketh in his heart so is he."
— PROVERBS 23:7

Control your thoughts and you control the material things that will eventually be manifested in your life. Self-control is one of the "fruits of the spirit."

IT IS WRITTEN:

"But the fruit of the Spirit is love, joy, peace, patience, kindness, goodness, faithfulness, gentleness, and self-control."
— GALATIANS 5:22-23(NIV)

Thoughts to meditate upon to Prepare for God's Abundant Life:

- Remember, lack of self-control is the basis of all sin.
- If you can control you, you can control your destiny.
- Discipline is self-control.
- Self-control is one of the "fruits of the spirit."

Your faith walk in life

No matter what the problem is or why you believe in God, it is having faith that will make the difference in your life. Faith accepts that God is in control, and that you can depend on Him.

It is written:

"...all things work together for good for those who love the Lord."
— ROMANS 8:28.

"Now faith is the substance of things hoped for, the evidence of things not seen."
— HEBREWS 11:1

"So then faith comes by hearing and hearing by the Word of God."
— ROMANS 10:17

"But without faith it is impossible to please Him, for He who comes to God must believe that He is, and that He is a rewarder of those who diligently seek Him."
— HEBREWS 11:6

God declares that He has a great future for you. The only way I know to find out, is to go to Him in prayer. He promised that He would listen to your prayers.

IT IS WRITTEN:

"Then you will call upon me and come and pray to me, and I will listen to you."

— JEREMIAH 29:12(NIV)

God wants you to have faith in all that you do. That means absolutely everything. The Bible says that anything you do without faith, is a sin. As it says in His Word, it is impossible to please Him without having faith.

God wants you to rely totally on Him for everything. He wants to be your sole Provider. God is not pleased when you try to be self-sufficient, for this implies that you do not need or have faith in Him.

When you do not use your faith, you do not please God. And, when you are able to accomplish goals and visions without using your faith in God, He does not get the glory.

In times of extreme pressure, God stretches our faith and deepens our dependence on Him. Without a strong abiding faith, you will quickly yield to temptation and fear.

IT IS WRITTEN:

"Behold the proud, His soul is not upright in Him, but the just shall live by faith."

— HABAKKUK 2:4

Remember, the more you read and study God's Word, the stronger your faith will grow. When hard times come, you will know that now is the time to use your faith in a different way. The more you use your faith, the greater it grows.

I have experienced setbacks several times in my life that were very disappointing. I became discouraged because of the setbacks. However, God got my attention quickly and I had to go to Him in prayer for help. God answered my prayers, I felt His presence, and it gave me peace.

You will come to realize that you cannot accomplish anything without God. God wants to be your source for everything. He does not want anyone or anything to take His place.

God knows how to get your attention. He will use whatever circumstance is available to bring you into a relationship with Jesus.

Many times, you might find yourself resisting His efforts to prune you. While pruning can be very uncomfortable and hurtful to you, it is designed to make you better.

Scientist tell us that there are more stars in the sky than there are grains of sand on all the beaches on earth, yet God calls all of them by name. Just as God knows each of us by name, he also knows what is best for each of us—we do not.

IT IS WRITTEN:

"He determines the number of the stars and calls them each by name."
— PSALM 147:4

"I've got my faith, and that's all I need."
— NELSON MANDELA

"I'm a man of faith. I have no army behind me except the "Army of God." There's nothing behind me except the faith and belief that the walls will come down."

— REV. LEON SULLIVAN

THOUGHTS TO MEDITATE UPON
TO PREPARE FOR GOD'S ABUNDANT LIFE:

- Practice using faith today.
- Ask God to stretch your faith.
- Use your faith in a different way.

What the bible says about money

As a believer, you cannot live simply with things that only money can buy. God made you this way. As a human being, you have a spirit and soul that requires the spiritual nurturing of God, namely, God's Word.

IT IS WRITTEN:

"Man shall not live by bread alone, but by every word that proceeds from the mouth of God."

— MATTHEW 4:4

"A feast is made for laughter, and wine makes merry; but money answers everything."

— ECCLESIASTES 10:19

Money is a tool that is used as a medium of exchange almost every place on earth. Without money, the economy would have to rely on the quality and efficacy of a barter system. Bartering is the exchange of one type of good for another type of good.

IT IS WRITTEN:

"The Bible tells us that we must 'not be given to wine, not violent, not greedy for money, but gentle, not quarrelsome, not covetous."

— 1 TIMOTHY 3:3

The Bible teaches that it is wrong to love money. "For the love of money is a root of all kinds of evil. For which some have strayed from the faith in their greediness and pierced themselves through with many sorrows."(1 Timothy 6:10) Yet, money is a very necessary commodity.

When money is sought after and spent because of greed and gluttony, it is sinful. When money is spent for the work of God, it is used as a means to an end—the building of God's kingdom. It can be used to build churches, to provide food and water for those in need, or to pay your pastors' salary.

All money flows to you from the creation and execution of ideas that come from your mind. Your thoughts are the seeds that will lead to the ideas that will lead to the flow of money you receive. There is more money generated from ideas than from pure labor.

"Money never starts an idea; it is the idea that starts the money.
— W.J. CAMERON

"Ideas are the beginning points of all fortunes."
— NAPOLEON HILL

"Thought is the original source of all wealth, all success, all material gain, all great discoveries and inventions, and of all achievement."
— CLAUDE M. BRISTOL

"A single idea — the sudden flash of a thought — may be worth a million dollars."

— ROBERT COLLIER

It is a sad fact that our school system does not teach students how to use their minds to create ideas that lead to wealth. For the most part, students are trained to be laborers and followers. This is the main reason that there is a lack of great ideas in the market place. Great ideas in the market place will assure a healthy economy and balanced budget. It is never a lack of money, so much as a lack of good ideas that stimulate new business opportunities.

As a believer, you have the privilege to go to God for answers. The Bible says that, "we have not because we ask not." (James 4:2b) God always has great ideas to share with you when you seek Him for godly ideas. Can you imagine the ideas that are available to you if you would just ask God, and believe that He will answer?

If at first you do not get what you want from God in prayer, continue to beseech Him until there is a breakthrough. Put action in your faith by believing that God will give you what you have asked for. God will not hold back on earnest requests you make of Him, if you go to Him with faith. Your request, however, must also be that which God wills for you.

IT IS WRITTEN:

"Seek God's kingdom and His righteousness, and all these things will be given to us as well."

— MATTHEW 6:33

You cannot do anything apart from God. You have no power except for the power God has given you If you desire money and wealth, it must come from God, His way. It is God who ultimately decides who gets wealth and keeps it. God has assigned some people to gather wealth for the sake of gathering and collecting it. but they will not keep it.

It is written:

"And you shall remember the Lord your God, for it is He who gives you power to get wealth, that He may establish His covenant which He swore to your fathers, as it is this day.
— Deuteronomy 8:18

"For God gives wisdom and knowledge and joy to a man who is good in His sight; but to the sinner He gives the work of gathering and collecting, that He may give to him who is good before God. This is vanity and grasping for the wind.
— Ecclesiastes 2:26

Thoughts to meditate upon to Prepare for God's Abundant Life:

- Pray and ask God for great ideas to make the world a better place.

- Know that God desires to give you what you ask, if your request is in His will.

- Never ask God for anything that is a selfish desire.

- Pray for those things that will aid others and you will be blessed in the process.

- Remember, success and money go hand-in-hand. You must remember to thank and honor God by using your wealth to spread the Word of God, and to share the love of God with others.

21

YOUR THOUGHTS AND IDEAS FOR WEALTH

"Thought is the original source of all wealth, all success, all material gain. All great discoveries and inventions, and all achievement."

— CLAUDE M. BRISTOL

Ideas are the backbone of our entire world. All prosperity and wealth come from a source of seeds of ideas you have. Everything man-made that you can see was once a thought or idea.

"Our greatest lack is not money for any undertaking, but rather ideas. If the ideas are good, cash will somehow flow to where it is needed."
— Robert H. Schuler

"A good idea plus capable men cannot fail; it is better than money in the bank."
— John G. Berry

"More gold has been mined from the thoughts of men than has ever been taken from the earth."
— Napoleon Hill

God gave you a mind that is rich with ideas. These ideas are for the good of humanity and not for any one individual. Each of you has the power to leave your mark on the earth, and to make it a better place to live.

God has goals for each of you to carry out while on earth. God plants ideas within your heart and mind in order to achieve His goals.

THOUGHTS TO MEDITATE UPON
TO PREPARE FOR GOD'S ABUNDANT LIFE:

- One idea can make a believer wealthy.
- Ideas are the mother to all inventions.
- An idea is priceless.

Discover who you are "In Christ"

There is more to you than your name. By telling me your name, I still do not know who you are. I just know your name, and nothing more.

When God wanted Moses to know who He was, He began with His lineage.

IT IS WRITTEN:

"I am the God of your father, the God of Abraham, the God of Isaac, and the God of Jacob."
— EXODUS 3:6

"And God said to Moses, 'I Am Who I Am."
— EXODUS 3:14

"You made us for Yourself, and our heart is restless until it rests in You."
— AUGUSTINE

"Therefore, if anyone is in Christ, he is a new creation; the old has gone, the new has come!"
— 2 CORINTHIANS 5:17(NIV)

God is the Creator of this universe and everything that is in it. This is what makes God who He is.

You should be identified and defined by your total make up, and not just your name. In order to know yourself, you should reflect upon:

- What makes you who you are?
- What do you believe about you?
- What does God say about you?

Once you understand these things, you will better understand and know the real you. This is called soul searching. Your success will determine how well you know you. If you do not fully know yourself, you are limited in what you believe you can accomplish.

We are all children of God. And, He has made each of us to be kingly.

IT IS WRITTEN:

"To Him who loved us and washed us from our sins
in His own blood, and has made us kings and priests to
His God and Father, to Him be glory and dominion forever
and ever. Amen. "

— REVELATION 1:5-6

Once you identify who and what God says you are, you should no longer have low self-esteem. As a believer, you should have a "can do" spirit at all times.

It is your responsibility to know what God says about you. Invest the time to learn who you are on a scriptural basis.

As a believer, you are an "Ambassador for Christ!"

"Now then, we are ambassadors for Christ, as though God were pleading through us: we implore you on Christ's behalf, be reconciled to God."

— 2 Corinthians 5:20

As a believer, you are righteous and without condemnation.

"Therefore, if anyone is in Christ, he is a new creation; the old has gone, the new has come!"
— 2 Corinthians 5:17(NIV)

"For He made Him (Christ) who knew no sin to be sin for us, that we might become the righteousness of God in Him."

— 2 Corinthians 5:21

THOUGHTS TO MEDITATE UPON
TO PREPARE FOR GOD'S ABUNDANT LIFE:

- You have been made righteous through the crucifixion of Jesus Christ.
- You are one of God's new creations.
- You have the mind of God, through your relationship with God.

Never quit on your dreams

God's plan and His purpose for you is acted upon and carried out through the dreams He has placed on your heart. Your desires, and God's desires for you should be the same.

When God wants something done, He just plants the thought in the mind of His believers. When you are in relationship with God, you will come to understand that the desires, thoughts, and ideas you have are those that God wants you to believe in.

Just as God created your thoughts and ideas, He also gave you the capacity to dream. Because God can control your dreams, He can manipulate the thoughts and ideas necessary for you to carry out His plan.

You should never give up on your dreams, and pursuit of God's purpose for you in life. When you abandon or quit pursuing your dreams, you are actually quitting on God, and the dreams He gave to you. Although you have the free will to quit, you are still subject to the plans He has for you.

We live in a world that is ruled by the Devil who is both an enemy of God and you, the believer. The Devil wants to block your dreams, discourage you, and destroy your faith in God as the source for your success. He wants you to abandon your dreams, and will try anything to make you lose faith and trust in God. The Devil is in the business of destroying your relationship with God.

It is written:

"The thief does not come except to steal, and to kill and to destroy."

— JOHN 10:10A

212

Thoughts to meditate upon to Prepare for God's Abundant Life:

- You should never consider quitting. You must persist until you succeed.
- The Scriptures teaches you to imitate God. Because God is not a quitter, you must never quit.
- The Devil will put thoughts in your mind that will tempt you into quitting.
- The Bible says, "resist the Devil and he will flee from you." (James 4:7)

You should have victory in everything

Think of anything you have ever tried to accomplish. Were you initially thinking success or failure? As a believer, you have the right to think victoriously as a result of your relationship with Jesus Christ. There can be no defeat in your life when you abide in God, and all God's Word abides in you.

When you understand God's plan for you, you must attach His purpose for you to your goals. The value placed on the goal and His purpose for you will help determine how persistent you are in reaching the goal. The bigger the "purpose" or intent of the goal, the greater the victory you and God will attain when you realize your goal. The average believer will want to quit on a dream if it is not valued highly.

The unbeliever cannot claim victory in Jesus Christ because there is no relationship. The unbeliever does not recognize Jesus as his Savior. In essence, He has rejected the Son of God. The unbeliever does not understand that it is God's Spirit that is the personal guarantee for the attainment of wonderful things by the believer. The unbeliever is on his own, without God's blessings.

Remember, victory comes from thinking "I will get what I want," not from thinking, "I'd like to have something." You see, "I will" is the strongest commitment you can make. When you think, "I will," your mind will perform two amazing acts—it will show you how to achieve your dreams, and it will supply the energy needed.

Your mental power is in the "I will" part of your mind. The deeper you fixate on the desires in your mind, the more certain you will get what you want.

Think, "I will" when you desire a new home. For a new business, think, "I will" make my business idea a reality. When you have "I will" and God embedded in your mind, heart, and soul you can easily achieve all that you desire in love, money, and relationships.

If you say, "I'll try," this can translate into "I may do it but I'm not sure I can do it. I may fail." But when you say "I will," this can translate into "In all my power, through Christ, I will make this happen. Nothing can stop me. I am in control. I see myself as having already accomplished this task."

I should note that there is no other qualification for success as important as having confidence in your ability to speak in front of a group of people, to command their attention, and to win them over to your point of view. Unfortunately, our educational system generally ignores two areas—how to build wealth, and the development of your ability to speak in front of a group of people to win them over to your point of view.

As a believer, you must be vigilant over whatever you desire—your goals and dreams. You must look for the outward sign that your desire is coming. You must pray for and claim your desire. To claim your desire is to state exactly what you want and to ask for it with authority. You have the right because you are a child of God.

Repeat this with authority, power and feeling, "This is mine and it is my divine right to have it. I will not do without it. I will be victorious." This is God's law and a promise of His Word.

IT IS WRITTEN:

"So I say to you, ask, and it shall be given to you; seek, and you will find; knock, and it will be opened to you."

— LUKE 11:9

THOUGHTS TO MEDITATE UPON
TO PREPARE FOR GOD'S ABUNDANT LIFE:

- Think victory in everything you do.
- Acknowledge God always, and He will direct your path.
- You must imitate God daily. This will give you the power to gain victory.
- Use the power in you to do things better each day.

Conclusion

Knowing God's Word is not enough to receive the promises He has for you. You must tap into His power through the Holy Spirit. Make your life count by doing something to positively affect the lives of others, and resolve to live a Holy life.

It is good to strive to do great things in life, but it requires power. Know that God has given all believers power. You must first believe that you have His power in order to use it. Know that you have the power to do great things in life.

As a believer, you should put your vision in writing. A vision in writing is a vision with power. If your vision is not in writing, it is only a wish. You will have a wish that has no power. Your wish is no more than a daydream.

Believe that you can do anything that God plans for you. Know that you have the attributes for success that God has given you.

Invest in the time to build a relationship with Him. Go to God in prayer. Learning to hear His voice, and recognizing the thoughts He gives to you takes time. He will communicate with you, and eventually you will learn to understand what He says to you. He will guide your steps along the right path for attaining success and wealth.

You must believe that God will never give up on you. He wants to give you the desires of your heart. However, He wants you to live a life that is pleasing to Him. To fear God and keep His commandments is only part of becoming a successful believer. Know that He also desires for you to have a Christ-like character and self-control. God wants you to attain everything you desire that is good for you, and that is within His will for you.

Finally, remember that it is only through obedience that you will receive His abundant blessings. Continue to study to show thyself acceptable unto the Lord, for you only get God's perspective when you know and understand His Word.

THOUGHTS TO MEDITATE UPON
TO PREPARE FOR GOD'S ABUNDANT LIFE:

- Pray and ask God for great ideas to make the world a better place.
- Know that God desires to give you what you ask, if your requests are in His will.
- Never ask God for anything that is a selfish desire.
- Pray for those things that will aid others and you will be blessed in the process.
- In everything that you do, do with the acknowledgement and power of God.
- Let God direct your steps.
- Commit to living a Holy life, for this is pleasing to God.

"He shall be like a tree planted by the rivers of water, That brings forth its fruit in its season, Whose leaf also shall not wither; And whatever he does shall prosper."

—PSALM 1:3

Bibliography

Brainy Media. *Brainy Quotes: Napoleon Hill.* 2009. http://www. brainyquote.com/quotes/authors/n/napoleon_hill_2.html (accessed July 27, 2009).

Churchill, Winston. *Inspirational Words of Wisdom: Winston Churchill Quotes.* http://www.wow4u.com/winston-churchill/index.html (accessed August 6, 2009).

Gibran, Kahlil. "The Prophet." *Google Books.* 1923. http://books. google.com/books?id=n5BlBsFbGOQC&pg=PR3&dq=gibran+on+childr en&source=gbs_selected_pages&cad=5 (accessed July 27, 2009).

Hill, Napoleon. *Think and Grow Rich.* New York, New York: Random House Publishing Group, 1960.

Microsoft Corporation. *Dictionary: Meditation.* 2009. http://encarta. msn.com/dictionary_/meditation.html (accessed July 13, 2009).

—. *Encarta MSN Dictionary: Plan.* 2009. http://encarta.msn.com/ dictionary_/plan.html (accessed August 1, 2009).

—. *msn. encarta, Dictionary: Patience.* 2009. http://encarta.msn. com/dictionary_1861724214/patience.html (accessed July 12, 2009).

NA. *Fortunate Sons.* February 23, 2007. http://www.snopes.com/ glurge/fortune.asp (accessed July 18, 2009).

Unknown. *Begum's Mind Science Page.* http://www.geocities.com/ athens/academy/4843/mindsc.htm (accessed June 30, 2009).

Wallenda, Tino. ""He Found Me" from Decision Magazine, a publicaton of the Billy Graham Evangelistic Association." *The Flying Wallendas Web site.* http://www.wallenda.com/clipping.html/he found me.htm (accessed July 25, 2009).

About the Author

Odell Young, Jr. has authored two books: **"Real Estate Investing for the Beginner" and "Getting Started in Real Estate."** These books became training manuals during his tenure as a trainer for the Georgia Real Estate Investors Association, the largest private real estate investors association in the United States. He served as a primary guest speaker for a GAREIA monthly meeting in 1998 to a standing room only attendance of more than five hundred real estate professionals. Mr. Young became one of the organizations' most sought-after motivational speaker and guest lecturer.

Odell has taught real estate investing in the private sector for more than nine years. His expertise and motivational skills have led to a multitude of appearances on radio and television shows. In addition, he has been invited to host several radio programs in real estate investing.

In November 1997, he founded Atlanta Metro Home Finders, Inc., a company that specialized in locating homes for apartment dwellers. His most recent venture was the purchase of a 3.5-acre shopping plaza in Riverdale, Georgia. His tenants included a Sprint cell tower and several businesses. Odell later sold this commercial property for a profit of over a quarter of a million dollars.

In the fall of October 2007, a spiritual transition occurred in Odell's life. God revealed to him that he was doing business the world's way rather than God's way. The business was brought to an end shortly after this revelation from God.

Odell had been teaching wealth building for financial independence since the beginning of his teaching career. He soon realized that God did not agree with the wealth building approach he had been teaching. He came to understand that "God wants His children to always rely on Him and not ourselves. When we rely on ourselves for success, God does not get the glory, and there are no permanent blessings in our business."

Since his spiritual transition, Odell has learned to do business God's way—that means putting Him first and acknowledging Him in all that he does. Mr. Young's spiritual walk has led him to completely trust and rely on God for everything now, and he now gives God the glory for all the successes and achievements in his life. **"Only God Can Give You the Power to Get Wealth"** is an outcome of the development of his relationship with God, and his spiritual journey into new business ventures—doing God's work and getting wealth God's way.

While real estate is still an avenue of interest, Odell spends most of his time developing relationships with pastors so that he can assist churches in meeting their financial needs, and help spread the gospel of our Lord Jesus Christ. The church's financial needs must be met in order for the community to prosper and serve the great needs of God's children.

Odell's goal is to help provide free health screening opportunities for church members in need. In addition, he plans to create and offer several wealth creation programs through the church that can improve the quality of life for pastors, church members, and residents of the local community.

His ultimate goal is to utilize his real estate background to forge opportunities for churches to expand their portfolios to include the acquisition of real estate and commercial business ventures(such as restaurant or hotel franchises). The acquisition of such ventures would enable churches to play a greater role in the economic development and revitalization of the communities they serve. Mr. Young believes that one of his God-given assignments is to help build an economic foundation and positive future for the youth in surrounding church communities.

Odell is a graduate of Morehouse College with a degree in Business Administration. He and his wife Delores reside in Palmetto, Georgia. They have been blessed with three wonderful children, Angela, DeAnn, and Kevin.